How to Buy and Sell Stocks Yourself:

Realize Family's Dreams and Invest Like A Billionaire

How to Buy and Sell Stocks Yourself:

Realize Family's Dreams and
Invest Like A Billionaire

Titus Gay

To order additional copies of this book, contact:
Xlibris LLC
1-888-795-4274
www.Xlibris.com
Orders@Xlibris.com
131668

Contents

One of the most popular trading site is Etrade

E trade.com
E trade official site
Open an account
Choose your Account
Complete investment account *Press continue*
To open an account
you need _ ss#

Your permanent address
Date of Birth
Employer name and address

Need help call—Etrade   1800-3872331
1888-639-4353

For trading cash account, most people we spoke with like cash account
because it is more simple to understand.

Easy Steps to Opening
An Online Stocks Account

Often times people think of the Stocks Market as the wealthy mans' playground, the truth is we all can play. It's easier than you think to create your own portfolio. With the internet, investment firms have made it very easy to open an online stocks account and begin trading. There is no longer a great need to have a stocks broker trading for you. Stocks trading sites give you all the information you need and with some time and add a little ingenuity you have an instant investor.

We want to assist you on your online investing journey. The information that we are providing will allow you to open, trade, and maintain your online trading account, in just a few simple steps. Before we begin, you must have internet access and a checking or savings account. We do not endorse any online trading companies. However, we have studies surveying people who trade online, with etrade.com and ameritrade.com are the most popular sites. Now Let's begin.

First things first, have all your personal information ready, bank/check book and relax. After getting on the computer and accessing the internet, please go to the online brokerage of your choice. Once you are on the site look for a tab that says **"open account"** and click on it. After clicking on that tab you will see that there are a few ways to set up an account {fill out the online application or download the application and mail it in}. The fastest and most common way is to fill out the online application. If you choose to apply online, [which is highly recommended] look for the tab online application or start and click on it. Read and follow the instructions carefully. On the following pages they will ask you several questions, beginning with your name, address, social security number, etc. Please be aware these sites are secure and so is your personal information, so don't be alarmed. After answering these questions, they will request your banking information. On average online brokerage accounts can be opened with $500-$1000. Once you make the transfer from your personal account to the online stocks account, you will receive a confirmation number. The setup is almost done, you will receive your account information. You must make a password and user ID, most often which will consist of both numbers and letters. Please make the user ID and password unique. Now your set up is complete. If you like, you can make sure the transaction is complete by calling the company {look for contact info tab} Now you are ready to begin trading.

Mailing in the application

Let us not forget there is another way to open an online stocks trading account (if you filled out the online application skip this part). The process is the same, until you get to the application don't fill it out, find the tab that states "download application" click it, print it, and fill it out. Look for the tab contact information, click it and write the mailing address for *new accounts.* The amount of money needed to open the account should be provided, if it is not call the company to find out. Once you have all the information, fill out the check and complete the application, mail it and you are done. You will be able to trade once the company receives your application and check. It may take a little time, please be patient, you are on your way.

Trading Stocks Online

You have completed opening your online account, wasn't that simple. Remember choose the online brokerage of your choice. Have your account information handy. Before we begin trading remember there is always a level of risk that comes with any investment (whether it's real estate or the stocks market). Please trade responsibly. With any project always give it due diligence.

When you are ready to purchase a **share** in a company, you will need the **symbol** for that company. If you don't have the symbol of the company, look for the Tab **symbol look up,** click it and type the name of the company in the space provide. Now you have the symbol, we advise you, to look for the tab **Quotes,** type the symbol in the space provided. On this page you will have company news, the price of the stocks per share, at that time (you need this info so you know how many shares you can buy). Now you have your symbol and your quote per share, you can begin trading with your online account.

We hope at this point you have done your research on the companies you want to invest in. Once you are on the brokerage website, look for a section or tab that says **"Trade"** and click on it. On the next page you must click on buying or selling at this point there is nothing in your **portfolio** click the buying tab. After clicking the tab buying, you will need the symbol for the company you are investing in. Type in the symbol and the amount of shares you want to purchase. Check all the information, if you a satisfied, click to **confirm order**. And you are done (if you like to buy more stocks in other companies just repeat the process).

You have made your first trade, and I know you're feeling good. The best thing about having an online stocks trading account, you can check your investments any time of the day. If you feel the need to buy and/or sell there is no need to reach a broker, it can be done in a few minutes. And most companies allow you to trade for as little as $7.99 per transaction (a lot less than 2-5% commission the broker usually takes per transaction).

We can't tell you how to maintain or monitor your account, however we can give you a few tips. When you access your online stocks trading account (after logging on the online brokerage site) there is a section or tab that says your account information. This is where you can see what companies you have brought or sold, how much you lost or gained and, when you purchased it and for how much and how much money you have available to purchase shares. You can also check your portfolio to see what companies you have invested in. Remember to watch the market. Looking at the history of the company is just one aspect, a very important one, however there are a few things that can affect a company's stocks value to go up or down. Fluctuation in a company can be caused by a number of things, a merger, a lawsuit, even war. That is why it's imperative to watch the financial news as well as your local and/or international news. It is also wise to watch a few stocks market television programs, to help you get familiar with the market and how it operates and to know what's going on.

In this book AASWM has provided you with over **180** companies to choose from. Our researchers have followed these companies and there have been progressing for several years. You must always remember there is a level of risk when investing, so please do your research and be cautious. We are excited to help you on your journey to financial success. Thank you for putting your confidence in AASWM. Good Luck!

Terms to know as an Investor

Stocks market

An organized market where brokers meet to buy and sell stocks and shares.

Portfolio

All the investments held by a person or organization.

Symbol lookup

Searching for a company's information.

IPO

A corporation's first offer to sell stocks to the public.

Quote

To state the current market price of a stocks, bond, or commodity.

Trade

The activity of buying and selling.

Ira

A plan that permits working people to invest money for retirement and pay no tax on the amount invested either at the time of investment or after retirement. Very little compared to other countries.

After Hours Trading

After-hours trading is the trading of securities, such as stocks and bonds, on organized markets and exchanges after regular business hours. These after-hours, electronic transactions explain why a security may open during regular business hours at a price that is different from the one it closed at the day before. Some interpret the level of activity and the direction the after-hours trading—up or down—as an early indicator of what may happen in the market the following day.

Brokerage Firms

Brokerage firms are licensed to buy and sell securities for clients and for their own accounts. Brokerage firms provide individual investors their link to the financial markets by employing brokers who carry out the investor's order to buy or sell securities.

The firm may be a huge, corporation with hundreds of brokers, a small partnership with only one broker or any size in between. A brokerage firm could also be a full-service firm, a discount firm or somewhere in between. Typically, larger firms, and full-service firms, provide an increasing range of financial services, including financial planning, asset management, and educational programs. In addition, many maintain research departments for their own and their clients' benefit. Other brokerage firms, such as online firms and discount firms, are increasingly providing their customers with a wealth of investment information on their website and encouraging their customers to trade electronically.

An investor should note that while online and discount brokerage firms may charge lower commissions than full-service brokerage firms to execute their buy and sell orders, those firms are also less likely to provide the range of services mentioned above. This may not be an issue for many investors as extensive information and online account access are now readily available. The individual investors' needs will dictate which services will be required.

Cash Accounts

Requiring that you pay for the securities transaction in full, this is the most common type of investment account. This account is used by customers who invest in securities using only the money they currently have available in their brokerage account.

Day Trading (Day Traders)

This is a trading strategy in which the investor buys then sells, or sells short then buys, the same security on the same day in an attempt to profit from small movements in the price of that security. The strategy is to take advantage of rapid price changes to make money quickly.

This is a legal investment strategy; however, it is also highly risky and should be reserved for more experienced investors. Most of us do not have the wealth or time to make money by day trading, much less the ability to sustain the devastating losses that it can bring.

Diversification (Diversified)

This is an investment strategy wherein the investor spreads their investment dollars among different markets, sectors, industries, and securities. By adopting this strategy the investor seeks to protect the value of their overall portfolio in the event that a single security, industry or market sector takes a serious downturn and drops in price. Studies have shown that diversification can help secure your investments against market and management risks without sacrificing the level of return desired.

Establishing a well-diversified portfolio will depend on the investor's age, assets, risk tolerance and investment goals. The securities mix that's right for you may include small-, medium-, and large-cap domestics stocks, stocks in multiple sectors or industries and international stocks.

ECN's (Electronic Communications Networks)

This technological advancement completes trade orders electronically, from start to finish, and maintains each order as part of an electronic record. When new orders are entered, the system automatically checks them against existing orders to see if there is a match—a buyer offering what a seller is asking. If there is a match, the system will execute the deal immediately without involving a specialist.

Since matches are made anonymously, large institutional investors have the ability to make trades without attracting attention or creating speculation about their possible motives. An additional advantage of the ECNs is that they make it easy to trade after-hours, when the markets are closed; however, ECNs are accessible only to its members.

IPO's (Initial Public Offerings)

As a company grows larger, it may decide to go public by issuing stocks, or adding shareholders, through an initial public offering (IPO). The purpose of issuing stocks and adding shareholders may be to raise capital, to provide liquidity for the existing shareholders, or a number of other reasons. When planning to issue an IPO the company must register its offering with the Securities and Exchange Commission (SEC). Typically, the company will work with an investment bank, which underwrites the offering by purchasing all of the shares at a predetermined price and then reselling them to the public in hopes of making a profit.

Limit Order

Limit orders allow the customer to specify the price at which he or she is willing to buy or sell a security. While limit orders can help investors avoid buying or selling security at an undesirable price, thereby protecting them from the possibility of rapid price changes, there is the risk that the limit order will not be executed (i.e., the market price may quickly surpass your limit before the order can be filled). In addition, some firms may charge you more for executing limit orders.

Liquidity

Liquidity refers to the ease with which an investment can be converted to cash. The more liquidity the investment is said to have, the easier it will be for the investor to convert it to cash.

Margin

Within a margin account, the margin is the portion of the purchase price that the customer must deposit into the account. This portion may also known as the customer's initial equity in the margin account.

Margin Account

This account allows the investor to increase their purchasing power by borrowing money from a brokerage firm to invest in securities. The money that the investor borrows must be repaid and the investor must possess collateral in their margin accounts in the form of securities in the event that they are unable to repay their brokerage firm. In the event that the investor is unable to pay the brokerage firm for a margin loss, the investor may be forced, with or without their knowledge, to liquidate the securities in their margin account. The investor's liability may also extend beyond the value of the securities in their margin account. In addition, the investor must pay applicable margin interest for borrowing the money from their brokerage firm. While buying securities on margin may equate to greater profits than an investor would received simply using their own resources, those profits must exceed the margin borrowing expenses in order for the investor to profit.

Buying on margin is risky and the investor should understand the principles and risks entirely before trading on margin.

Margin Account with Options

This is a margin account with the opportunity to purchase options. By purchasing an option, the investor has the right to buy or sell a specific security at a specific price, called a strike price, during a predetermined period of time.

If the investor buys an option to buy, known as a call, they will pay a one-time premium—a fraction of the cost of the actual transaction. For example, an investor might buy a call option giving them the right to buy 400 shares of a particular stocks at a strike price of $99 a share when that stocks is currently trading at $85 a share. In the event that the prices goes higher than the strike price, the investor would want to exercise the option and buy the stocks at the lower cost per share, or even trade that option with someone, in either case experiencing a profit. If the stocks price didn't go higher than the strike price, the investor would simply choose not to exercise the option and that option would expire. The only money that investor would have lost was the money paid for the premium.

Similarly, an investor may purchase a put option, which gives them the right to sell the security to the person who sold them the option. In this case, the investor would exercise the option if the market price dropped below the strike price.

Trading in options is a risky investment opportunity and should be reserved for more experienced investors.

Margin Call

In a margin account if the investor falls below the margin requirements, they may be subject to a margin call wherein the brokerage firm asks for additional funds to be added to the investors account. In the event that the investor is unable to pay the brokerage firm for a margin call, the brokerage firm may sell part or all of the securities held in the margin account, with or without the investor's knowledge, in order to make up the value and meet the margin limit requirements.

Margin calls can occur suddenly and investors should understand fully the financial impact that trading on margin can have on the value of their accounts.

Market Order

This is an order in which the investor instructs his or her brokerage firm to buy or sell as security at the current market price, ideally as soon as possible. Unless the investors specifies otherwise, a broker will enter the order as a market order.

The advantages of a market order are that the investor is almost always guaranteed that their order will be executed (as long as there are willing buyers and sellers) and a market order is typically less expensive than a limit order.

The disadvantage of a market order is that the investor has no control over the price at which their order will ultimately be filled. If the price of the security is moving quickly and there is a delay in the execution of the market order, then the price at which the investor buys or sells the security may be quite different than what they expected with the market order was originally placed.

Minimum Maintenance Requirement

With regards to trading on margin the amount that an investor can borrow is limited by both the Federal Reserve Board and the specific brokerage firm used. Generally, there are two requirements—how much margin an investor can use initially in the margin account and then how much margin they can have once the initial transaction has been executed. While each brokerage firm creates its own requirements, typically, in the initial transaction, 50% of the purchase price of any security can be margin. Once the initial transaction has been executed the maintenance margin account requirement is usually much lower, often around 25%. Investors should consult with their individual brokerage firms to determine the initial and ongoing maintenance margin requirements.

Mutual Funds

Mutual funds pool money from several investors (individual and/or institutions) and invest the pooled money in various types of investments (i.e., stocks, bonds, specific industries, etc.). Investment decisions are based on the common financial goals of the investors. The suitability of a particular mutual fund depends on the types and nature of the fund's investments and the amount of diversification. Not all mutual funds are equal and investors need to determine if the goals of a particular mutual fund match their own personal financial goals.

The advantages of mutual funds are diversification, liquidity, and professional management. By pooling money from many investors, individual investors are able to own more securities than they might be able to afford on their own; therefore, owning a mutual fund may offer the investor instant holdings in several different companies. In terms of liquidity, mutual fund investments can be converted to cash upon request. And rather than managing your investments yourself, a mutual fund allows you to turn over the responsibility to a "professional."

Online Broker Ratings (ratings/rankings)

In general, online brokerage ratings indicate the level of customer service or satisfaction with the online brokerage firm. There are several sources of online broker ratings and each may use different criteria in their ratings. In addition, the online broker ratings sources are not regulated entities. Investors should keep in mind that while a brokerage firm may be ranked #1, that is in terms of customer satisfaction and it does not mean that they will have a better chance of making you money.

Prospectus

A written, legal document outlining the investment offered for sale. A prospectus provides all of the material information about an offering of securities, and serves as the primary sales tool of the company issuing the security and broker-dealers who sell the security.

The prospectus is also serves as written proof that the investor was given all the material facts as they are set out in the prospectus. It is for this reason that investors should be certain that they understand the information contained the prospectus.

Stop Loss Order

A stop loss order instructs a broker to sell a specific stocks it if falls to a certain price. This is a useful tool in preventing investor losses. For example, you buy ABC Company at $100 a share and you instruct your broker to sell if it falls to $90 a share. On a given day the stocks falls to $70 a share. Your broker sold your shares when they reach $90 thereby saving you an additional $20 per share loss on your investment.

The suitability of an investment depends on whether the investment is consistent with the person's investing objectives and profiles (age, financial status, long-term goals, income, current financial status, etc.). Investment advisors and brokers giving investment advice are required by law to ensure that their recommendations are suitable for the investor. To help these financial professionals make appropriate recommendations an investor should provide honest and accurate information to that professional.

Stocks

Stocks represent individual ownership in a company. A share of stocks is equivalent to a proportional share of ownership in a company. The goal of stocks ownership is to see the value of the company increase over time. As the value of the company changes, the value of the share in that company rises and falls.

Taxable versus Tax-Deferred

A taxable investment refers to investments in which the earnings will be taxed as they are received. A tax-deferred investment refers to investments in which the tax is not paid as earning are received but will be due when the untaxed money is withdrawn from that tax-deferred account.

Main Stocks Exchanges

American Stocks Exchange (AMEX)
London Stocks Exchange
NASDAQ
New York Stocks Exchange (NYSE)
Tokyo Stocks Exchange
S&P 500 Index
Russell 3000
Dow Jones Industrial Average

Steps to take in consideration

Start small

Never put your entire life savings into an online account.

Start with a small sum, which will be easier to handle and keep track of.

Once you feel you got the hang of things, you can decide to add more money to your online account.

Be diverse

Many investors tend to concentrate on large-cap domestic stocks.

These stocks should make up part of your portfolio, not all of it!

Develop a well-balanced portfolio of stocks, bonds, and cash.

Don't run away from mutual funds

Most investors have mutual funds for a good reason. They don't have the expertise to make their own investments calls on individual stocks.

Sometimes investors may get too preoccupied with work, the family and other concerns to spend every minute watching the market.

So keep your mutual funds; it's an unwise move for you to cash out your long-term fund holdings, but you can start "playing the market" in individual stocks!

Costs may not always be noticeable

Even if online brokerage costs are lower than other full-service brokers, they can still add up, especially if you do a lot of buying and selling.

Online brokerages firms also impose a number of other fees and charges that you should look over closely.

The federal capital gains tax is also something with which you must reckon. Before you start buying and selling stocks or mutual funds online on a large scale, you should give careful thought to what the tax bite would be.

Make orders work for you

If you are going to do your own investing online, you need to learn how to use the tools to avoid potentially steep losses and to buy or sell a stocks at attractive prices. Here are three "orders" that you should use to your advantage: Market order, limit order, and stop-loss order.

Mind those market orders

This book was created to help you understand how easy it is to trade on the stocks market yourself; to let the world know that the stocks market is not just for the rich.

The stocks market has made many people rich and now it is your turn to be a millionaire

Our survey shows that most of the stocks traders we spoke with like to use E trade.com or TD Ameritrade.com as there trading site.

When buying stocks always buy low and sell high. For example AZO or Auto Zone, an auto parts store, their stocks goes high every year before the winter starts. As a result you buy the stocks in the middle of winter because most people already bought their auto parts and repaired their cars. As a result auto parts sales will slow down and stocks prices will drop then this would be the time to buy. You would want to check all seasonal stocks to see the months they go up and down. I recommend Auto Zone as one of the best stocks to buy

Limit orders are often used an, investor may pay a dollar for a stocks. If no limit is placed, the trade is considered to be a market order.

Placing a market order means you won't necessarily get the price you see when you buy or sell online. Here's how that works: an investor places an order for a fast-moving stocks at $10 share price, but the order does not reach the market until the stock's price is at $15 a share.

Problems are inevitable

There will be times when you can't access your account. You might be away from your computer when the market makes a major move.

Your Internet connection could be down. The online brokerage firm's server could crash due to heavy trading, unexpected software glitches or a natural calamity.

Know about the firm's alternative trading options just in case. This could include automated telephone trading or calling a broker.

Information is power

If you are going to buy and sell individual stocks online, it is your duty to keep as well informed as possible about what is going on with the company. Don't just settle for the hype hot stocks!

Go to the company's Web site and download its prospectus.

Check out the company's publicly.

Take advantage of free services like automatic e-mail messages whenever there is news about your stocks.

What is a Penny Stocks

Many people that don't know much about the stocks market will say a penny stocks is a stocks that cost a penny a share

But according to the Securities and Exchange Commission (SEC) any stocks under $5 is a penny stocks, definition can vary some traders set the cut-off point at $3 while other would say less than one dollar. Penny stocks are much riskier than regular stocks

Be careful with penny stocks companies that have little or no information. Companies that are on the OTCBB and pink sheets do not go through regulation with the (SEC) like the large companies. OTCBB and pink sheets do not have to fulfill minimum standard requirements to remain on the RX change that is why you will find penny stocks on this exchange. Some people became millionaires from penny stocks but you have to be very observing and careful

Oil stocks can make you millions

Oil prices are expected to go to five dollars and I know that oil stocks usually goes down when the price of oil is low. This is the time to buy, oil stocks will go up quickly when there is disturbance in the Middle East. If Israel goes to war with its Arab Neighbors, the price of oil could go very high. The penny oil stocks can make you very rich check my oil stocks list sometimes these oil stocks double and triple.

Unrest in the Middle East can make you rich may God bless and heal the families of 911 but on 911 and months after many of the stocks lost more than half their value. What I am trying to say is every big disaster most stocks will come tumbling down therefore that is the time to buy because history shows that the stocks always goes back up and sometimes more than triple the original amount.

Legally Crooked Oil Companies

Oil companies are making Billions and the consumers are unhappy, but if you can't beat them join them read page 57 to 58.

It tell you the best oil and gas stocks to buy, some oil stocks double and triple every year, you buy the oil stocks at its lows and sell at its highs in November & December many oil companies their stocks go low and that is the time to buy

In February & March the oil stocks mostly go high, then you sell. Some times these months that I mention don't always go in order with the stocks going low and high, but the idea is to buy low and sell high, which every month it occurs. The big oil lie, people are saying that oil companies would use every lying excuse to raise the price of oil for example = Trouble in the Middle East

The Arabs are fighting it may cause oil ships to be in danger so the price of oil will go up or our refinery not working and less oil are being produce, so the price of oil will go up

The Government makes more money also, I must say to the consumers again join the oil companies buy their stocks and get even.

Companies with Political ties can make a Financial difference

Knowing more about the Government and Politician, what they do, who are their friends and what companies they have ties with can make a difference in the stocks that you buy, for example—former vice president Dick Chaney work for Haliburton he also get a pension from that company He have very close ties to that company. When George Bush became president my son told me to buy Haliburton stocks but I did not give his words any attention to my amazement that stocks went from $16 a share to $60 a share in a very short time. One of the reasons for that stocks to move so quickly is because the Bush and Dick Chaney Administration allowed billions of dollars in no bid contracts to go to Haliburton. You must watch out for companies that get Government contracts some stocks can double with Government and State contracts.

See what stocks the Billionaires Are buying and selling

In most cases if you do what the billionaires are doing chances are you will make money check the stocks market news and the internet for what stocks the billionaires are buying and selling I bought some shares in Circuit City years ago but when I saw the world richest man sell his shares in Circuit City I also bail out. Guess what happened to Circuit City? They went under shortly after. The world richest man is Carlos Simms (Bill Gates)?

Red alert   =   check stocks to see when it is at its lowest and highest, check the debt of the company.
Check   =   what cash they have on hand
Check   =   what money is owed to banks (mortgage companies)
Check   =   If customers are increasing
Stay away   =   From companies that have a lot of debt

A $25.000 Investment Can reap a Harvest of 250.000 in five years With These Stocks

Buying high quality stocks like—Bidu—priceline Google—Intel—Caterpillar. Or higher risk stocks

That call for caution and carefulness = like

Lucas Energy (LEI) Hercules offshore (Hero)

Radian Group Inc (RDN) Sirius XM Radio (Siri)

Unify (UNFY)

These stocks are cheap but you remember to always give higher risk stocks a lot more attention and it is not advisable to invest too much money in high risk stocks These stocks can sometimes double and triple in value in 1 year look for these stocks at its lows and buy and sell when it goes high remember always type in the symbol of the company when you go on your trading site, for example Ford Motor Co, the symbol is F

$HOT $tock$

These stocks that we brought to you, continues to make money in the stocks market and shows future growth.

- **Ebay (EBAY)**
- eBay Inc. has developed a web-based community in which buyers and sellers are brought together in an auction format to buy and sell items

WFMI—Whole Foods Market Inc.

- **Pro Gamble (PG)**
- PG manufactures and markets more than 250 products to consumers in throughout the world. Business categories are Baby and Family Care, Fabric and Home Care, Beauty Care, Health Care and Food and Beverage.

- **Exxon Mobil (XOM)**
- XOM is engaged in the exploration, production, manufacture, transportation and sale of crude oil, natural gas, and petroleum products, and the manufacture of petrochemicals, packaging films and specialty chemicals.

- **AMERICAN EXPRESS CO (Axp)**
- American Express and its subsidiaries provide travel-related services, financial advisory services and international banking services worldwide.

- **BOEING CO (Ba)**
  BA develops and produces jet transports, military aircraft and space and missile systems through 4 segments: commercial airplanes, military aircraft and missiles, space and communications and BCC.

- **Caterpillar (Cat)**
- CAT manufactures and markets construction and mining equipment, diesel and natural gas engines and industrial turbines, and also provides financing and insurance services.

- **Citigroup (C)**
- C provides financial services, including banking, insurance and investment services, to consumer and corporate customers.

- **Coca-Cola (Ko)**
- The Coca-Cola Company is a manufacturer, distributor and marketer of soft drink concentrates and syrups, & also markets & distributes juice and juice-drink products.

- **Disney, Walt (Dis)**
- The Walt Disney Company is a diversified worldwide entertainment company, operating in four segments: Media Networks, Parks and Resorts, Studio Entertainment and Consumer Products.

- **CHINA PETROLEUM & CHEM ADR (snp)**
- China Petroleum & Chemical is engaged in the refining and distribution of gasoline, diesel and jet fuel, the production and distribution of petrochemicals

- **AMERICAN EXPRESS CO (Axp)**
- American Express and its subsidiaries provide travel-related services, financial advisory services and international banking services worldwide.

- **BOEING CO (Ba)**
- BA develops and produces jet transports, military aircraft and space and missile systems through 4 segments: commercial airplanes, military aircraft and missiles, space and communications and BCC.

- **Caterpillar (Cat)**
- CAT manufactures and markets construction and mining equipment, diesel and natural gas engines and industrial turbines, and also provides financing and insurance services.

- **Citigroup (C)**
- C provides financial services, including banking, insurance and investment services, to consumer and corporate customers.

- **Coca-Cola (Ko)**
- The Coca-Cola Company is a manufacturer, distributor and marketer of soft drink concentrates and syrups, & also markets & distributes juice and juice-drink products.

- **Disney, Walt (Dis)**
- The Walt Disney Company is a diversified worldwide entertainment company, operating in four segments: Media Networks, Parks and Resorts, Studio Entertainment and Consumer Products.

- **CHINA PETROLEUM & CHEM ADR (snp)**
- China Petroleum & Chemical is engaged in the refining and distribution of gasoline, diesel and jet fuel, the production and distribution of petrochemicals

- **Horizon Financial (Hrzb)**
- Horizon Financial Corp. is a bank holding company for Horizon Bank, a state-chartered, FDIC-insured stocks savings bank.

- **National City Corp (NCC)**
- NCC is a regional bank holding company operating commercial banks with offices in OH, MI, PA, KY, IN and IL.

- **Wgnb Corp (Wgnb)**
- WGNB Corp. is the bank holding company of the West Georgia National Bank, a full-service commercial bank.

- **Yadkin Valley Bk (Yavy)** not available

- **AIG (AIG)**
  American International Group is a holding company engaged in insurance and insurance-related activities in the U.S. & abroad.

- **Alcoa (AA)**
- Alcoa, Inc. is an integrated aluminum company producing and selling aluminum, semi-fabricated and finished aluminum products and alumina.

- **ALTRIA GROUP INC (Mo)**
- Altria Group is a holding company whose principal subsidiaries are engaged in the manufacture and sale of various consumer products, including cigarettes, packaged & processed foods, and beverages.

- **Horizon Financial (Hrzb)**
- Horizon Financial Corp. is a bank holding company for Horizon Bank, a state-chartered, FDIC-insured stocks savings bank.

- **National City Corp (NCC)**
- NCC is a regional bank holding company operating commercial banks with offices in OH, MI, PA, KY, IN and IL.

- **Wgnb Corp (Wgnb)**
- WGNB Corp. is the bank holding company of the West Georgia National Bank, a full-service commercial bank.

- **Yadkin Valley Bk (Yavy)** not available

- **AIG (AIG)**
- American International Group is a holding company engaged in insurance and insurance-related activities in the U.S. & abroad.

- **Alcoa (AA)**
- Alcoa, Inc. is an integrated aluminum company producing and selling aluminum, semi-fabricated and finished aluminum products and alumina.

- **ALTRIA GROUP INC (Mo)**
- Altria Group is a holding company whose principal subsidiaries are engaged in the manufacture and sale of various consumer products, including cigarettes, packaged & processed foods, and beverages.

- **AMERICAN EXPRESS CO (Axp)**
- American Express and its subsidiaries provide travel-related services, financial advisory services and international banking services worldwide.

- **BOEING CO (Ba)**
- Bailey develops and produces jet transports, military aircraft and space and missile systems through 4 segments: commercial airplanes, military aircraft and missiles, space and communications and BCC.

- **Caterpillar (Cat)**
- CAT manufactures and markets construction and mining equipment, diesel and natural gas engines and industrial turbines, and also provides financing and insurance services.

- **Citigroup (C)**
- C provides financial services, including banking, insurance and investment services, to consumer and corporate customers.

- **Coca-Cola (Ko)**
- The Coca-Cola Company is a manufacturer, distributor and marketer of soft drink concentrates and syrups, & also markets & distributes juice and juice-drink products.

- **Disney, Walt (Dis)**
- The Walt Disney Company is a diversified worldwide entertainment company, operating in four segments: Media Networks, Parks and Resorts, Studio Entertainment and Consumer Products.

- **Du point (DD)**
- E.I. DuPont de Nemours and Company is a global science and technology company with operations in high-performance materials, specialty chemicals, pharmaceuticals and biotechnology.

- **Exxon Mob (Xom)**
- XOM is engaged in the exploration, production, manufacture, transportation and sale of crude oil, natural gas, and petroleum products, and the manufacture of petrochemicals, packaging films and specialty chemicals.

- **Gen Elec (Ge)**
- GE is a diversified industrial corporation whose products include appliances, lighting products, aircraft engines and plastics. GE also provides television, cable, internet, distribution, engineering & financial services.

- **Gen Motors (Gm)**
- General Motors Corp. designs, manufactures and markets automobiles, trucks and related parts, designs and manufactures locomotives and heavy-duty transmissions and operates a financial services and insurance company.

- **Hewl-pack (Hpq)**
- Hewlett-Packard Company is a global provider of computing and imaging solutions for business and home, focused on capitalizing on the opportunities of the Internet and the proliferation of electronic services.

- **Home Depot (Hd)**
- The Home Depot owns and operates 1,471 do-it-yourself warehouse retail stores offering building materials, home improvement products and related furnishings.

- **Untd Tech (Utx)**
- UTX has four principal operating segments: Otis (elevators and escalators), Carrier (heating, ventilating & air conditioning systems), Pratt & Whitney (aircraft engines and space propulsion), & Flight Systems (helicopters electrical systems).

- **Verizon (Vz)**
- Verizon is engaged in the provision of communications services, primarily wireline and wireless communications in the Americas, Europe, Asia and the Pacific.

- **Wal-mart (Wmt)**
- Wal-Mart Stores, Inc. operates discount department stores, warehouse membership clubs and superstores.

- **PHELPS DODGE CORP (pd)**
- PD operates Phelps Dodge Mining Co. (involved in copper operations-including mining, concentrating, smelting & refining) & Phelps Dodge Inds. (manufactures engineered products for the transportation, energy & telecommunications inds.).

- **STATOIL ASA SPON ADR (sto)**
- Statoil ASA is the largest integrated oil and gas company in Scandinavia, producing oil and gas from the Norwegian Continental Shelf and other regions, and has a 50% interest in a retail gasoline business.

- **CONOCOPHILLIPS (cop)**
- ConocoPhillips is an integrated global energy company with five operating segments: exploration and production, midstream, refining and marketing, chemicals and emerging businesses.

- **BLDRS EMERGING MKTS 50 ADR FD (adre)**
- not available

- **Merck (mrk)**
- Merck & Co., Inc. is a pharmaceutical company that discovers, develops, produces & markets human/animal health products and services.

- **Microsoft (Msft)**
- Microsoft Corporation develops, manufactures, licenses & supports a range of software products, including scalable operating systems, server applications, worker productivity applications and software development tools.

- **Pfizer (Pfe)**
- Pfizer Inc. is a global pharmaceutical and consumer products company that discovers, develops, manufactures and markets medicines for human and animal indications.

- **Proc Gamble (Pg)**
- PG manufacturers and markets more than 250 products to consumers in throughout the world. Business categories are Baby and Family Care, Fabric and Home Care, Beauty Care, Health Care and Food and Beverage.

- **Sbc Comm (Sbc)**
- SBC is a holding company whose subsidiaries provide wireline and wireless telecommunications services and equipment, directory advertising, and cable television services.

- **3M Co. (MMM)**
- 3M Co. manufactures and markets pressure-sensitive adhesive tapes, abrasives and specialty chemicals. 3M also markets electrical & telecommunication products, medical devices, office supplies and major automotive parts.

- **Honey well (Hon)**
- HON is a diversified technology and manufacturing company, serving customers worldwide with aerospace products and services, control technologies, automotive products, power generation systems, chemicals, fibers and other materials.

- **IBM (Ibm)**
- IBM provides customer solutions through the use of advanced information technology. These solutions include technologies, systems, products, services, software and financing.

- **Intel (Intc)**
- INTC is a maker of semiconductor chips, supplying the computing and communications industries with chips, boards, systems and software that are integral in computers, servers and networking and communications products.

- **Johnson J (JNJ)**
- Johnson & Johnson is a manufacturer of health care products serving the consumer, pharmaceutical and professional markets.

- **Jp morg ch (Jpm)**
- JPMorgan Chase & Co. conducts business in two broad spheres of activity: global financial services and retail banking.

- **McDonalds (Mcd)**
- McDonald's Corp. develops, operates, franchises and services a worldwide system of restaurants which prepare, assemble, package and sell a limited menu of value-priced foods.

- **Du point (DD)**
- E.I. DuPont de Nemours and Company is a global science and technology company with operations in high-performance materials, specialty chemicals, pharmaceuticals and biotechnology.

- **Exxon Mob (Xom)**
- XOM is engaged in the exploration, production, manufacture, transportation and sale of crude oil, natural gas, and petroleum products, and the manufacture of petrochemicals, packaging films and specialty chemicals.

- **Gen Elec (Ge)**
- GE is a diversified industrial corporation whose products include appliances, lighting products, aircraft engines and plastics. GE also provides television, cable, internet, distribution, engineering & financial services.

- **Gen Motors (Gm)**
- General Motors Corp. designs, manufactures and markets automobiles, trucks and related parts, designs and manufactures locomotives and heavy-duty transmissions and operates a financial services and insurance company.

- **Hewl-pack (Hpq)**
- Hewlett-Packard Company is a global provider of computing and imaging solutions for business and home, focused on capitalizing on the opportunities of the Internet and the proliferation of electronic services.

- **Home Depot (Hd)**
- The Home Depot owns and operates 1,471 do-it-yourself warehouse retail stores offering building materials, home improvement products and related furnishings.

- **Bank of America Corp (Bac)**
- BAC provides a diversified range of banking and certain non-banking financial services and products through its various subsidiaries.

- **Bell south corp (bls)**
- BellSouth Corporation is a communications services company that serves over 45 million local, long distance, Internet and wireless customers in the United States and 13 other countries.

- **Cardinal Health inc (cah)**
- CAH is a holding company that provides products and services to healthcare providers and manufacturers to help them improve the efficiency and quality of healthcare.

- **Duke energy corp (duk)**
- Duke Energy Corporation is an integrated energy company and a leading domestic gatherer and processor of natural gas and develops, constructs and operates energy facilities worldwide.

- **Eaton vnce Sr Inco (Evf)** not available

- **General Mills (gis)**
- General Mills, Inc. is a producer of packaged consumer foods, including, cereals, desserts, flour and baking mixes, dinner & side dish products, snack products, beverages, yogurt products and foodservice products.

- **Greenbrier Cos (Gbx)**
- GBX supplies transport equipment & services to railroad & related industries. GBX is also engaged in complementary leasing & services activities.

- **Burlington Resources (BR)**
- Burlington Resources Inc. is a holding company engaged, through its subsidiaries, in the exploration, development, production and marketing of crude oil and natural gas.

- **Eog Resources (EOG)**
- EOG is engaged in the exploration, development, production, and marketing of natural gas and crude oil, primarily in major producing basins in the U.S., as well as in Canada, Trinidad, & the U.K.

- **Auto Nation (AN)**
- AutoNation, Inc. is an automotive retailer. AN's business consists primarily of the sale, financing and servicing of new and used vehicles.

- **Hercules (HPC)**
- HPC manufactures specialty chemicals for industries such as pulp and paper, personal care, paints and coatings, adhesives and pharmaceuticals.

- **Schlumberger (SLB)**
- Schlumberger Limited is an oilfield services company that supplies technology, project management and information solutions that aim to optimize performance for customers working in the international oil and gas industry.

- **Prolong intl corp (PRL)**
- PRL manufactures, sells and distributes a patented complete line of high-performance lubricants and appearance products.

- **Teletouch Comm Inc (TLL)**
- Teletouch Communications provides paging, two-way mobile communications services

- **Baker Hughes (BHI)**
- BHI is engaged in the oilfield and process industry segments. BHI also manufactures and sells other products and provides services to industries that are not related to the oilfield or continuous process industries.

- **Xto Energy (XTO)**
- XTO is engaged in the acquisition, development, exploitation & exploration of oil & gas producing properties and in the production, processing and transportation of oil & natural gas.

- **Walgreen (WAG)**
- Walgreen Company is principally engaged in the retail drugstore business.

- **KB Home (KBH)**
- KB Home is a builder of single-family homes with domestic operations in the United States and international operations in France.

- **Centex (CTX)**
- CTX operates in five principal business segments: Home Building, Financial Services, Construction Products, Construction Services and Investment Real Estate.

- **Pulte Homes (PHM)**
- Pulte Homes, Inc. is a holding company whose subsidiaries are engaged in homebuilding and financial services businesses.

- **Anadarko Petroleum (APC)**
- Anadarko Petroleum Corp. is engaged in the production exploration, development, production, and marketing of natural gas, crude oil, condensate and natural gas liquids.

Hot Stocks

- **Unify (Unfy)**
- Unify Corp. develops, markets and supports Internet application server solutions that enable IT organizations to deliver e-commerce applications by integrating enterprise, custom built, and packaged applications with the Internet.

- **Hasbro Inc (HAS)**
- HAS designs, manufactures and markets a diverse line of toy products & related items including games, preschool toys, dolls, plush products & infant products, and licenses various property rights.

- **Nucor (NUE)**
- Nucor Corporation and its subsidiaries are engaged in the manufacture and sale of steel products, including hot-rolled, cold-rolled sheet, galvanized sheet, cold finished and more.

- **Auto Desk (ADSK)**
- Autodesk, Inc. is engaged in the development and marketing of design and drafting software and multimedia tools, primarily for the business and professional environment.

- **Bausch & Lomb (BOL)**
- BOL develops, manufactures and markets healthcare products for the eye in five business segments: lens care, pharmaceuticals, cataract and vetreoretinal and refractive.

- **Aes (AES)**
- The AES Corp. operates and owns a diverse portfolio of electric power plants.

- **Apollo Group (APOL)**
- Apollo Group is a provider of higher education programs for working adults. APOL offers its services at 82 campuses and 137 learning centers in 39 states, Puerto Rico and British Columbia.

Red Hot Stocks

Buy Low Sell High

Symbols

BIDU   -   BAIDU Inc
SINA   -   SINA Corp
M.C.D.   -   McDonald
Pcln   -   Priceline.com
GooG   -   Google
AApl   -   Apple
AMZn   -   Amazon
AZo   -   Autozone
Cat   -   Caterpillar
RDN   -   Radian Group Inc

PENNY Stocks That goes wild

Symbols

SIRI	-	Sirius XM Radio Inc.com
(Unfy) DAEG	-	Daegis Inc
SSN	-	Samson Oil & Gas LTD ✓
LEI	-	Lucas Energy Inc ✓
JASO	-	JA-Solar Holding Co
Ivan	-	Ivanhoe Energy Inc ✓
HERO	-	Hercules Offshore Inc ✓
NSRS	-	North Springs' Res Corp
BWEN	-	Broadwind Energy Inc
Royl	-	Royal Energy Oil & Gas Company ✓
R D N	-	Radian Group Inc—We believe this stocks will triple in one year

↕

R.D.N no longer a penny stocks this stocks have triple while I was writing this book

This stocks is hot

Penny stocks listings

A penny stocks is low-priced, typically selling for less than $4 doll

A share, and is not listed on a major exchange such as the New York Stocks Exchange. Also, penny stocks are popular among speculators.

Some of the Penny stocks companies do not give information about their company. As it should be.

INSM	-	INSMED INC		
MBND	-	MULTIBAND Corp		
RBG	-	REBGOLD ORD		
INFO	-	METRO ONE TELE COMM INC		
BMGP		BIOMAGNETICS DIAGNOSTICS CORP COM	OTC Pink—Limited	Common Stocks
BSTK		BRITE STRIKE TACTICAL ILLUMINA COM NEW	OTC Pink—Limited	Common Stocks
CTTG		CANADIAN TCTCL TRNNG ACDMY INC COM	OTC Pink—No Information	Common Stocks
CEMI		CHEMBIO DIAGNOSTICS INC COM NEW	NASDAQ	Common Stocks
CHDP		CHINA DAQING M&H PETROLEUM INC COM	OTC Pink—No Information	Common Stocks
CTXIF		CHINA LINEN TEXTILE IND LTD SHS NEW	OTCQB	Common Stocks
LBIX	-	LEADING BRANDS		
DAKO		DAKOTA GOLD CORP COM NEW	OTCBB—OTCQB	Common Stocks
DAKP		DAKOTA PLAINS HLDGS INC COM	OTCBB—OTCQB	Common Stocks

	Symbol	Name	Exchange	Security Type
	URXED	DAKOTA TERR RESOURCE CORP COM	OTCQB	Common Stocks
	AEZ	- AETERNA ZENTARIS		
	LNGYF	- LNG ENERGY LTD		
	ICAD	- CAD INC		
	TDCP	3DICON CORP COM NEW	OTCQB	Common Stocks
	ADSI	ADS TACTICAL INC COM	NYSE	Common Stocks
	Symbol	Name	Exchange	Security Type
	EGHA	8888 ACQUISITION CORP COM PAR $.0001	OTC Pink—No Information	Common Stocks
	ACLD	ACQUIRE LTD COM	OTC Pink—No Information	Common Stocks
✓	AQSP	ACQUIRED SALES CORP COM NEW	OTCQB	Common Stocks
	IVAN	- IVANHOE ENERGY		
	AEGW	ALTER ENERGY GROUP N A INC COM	Grey Market	Common Stocks
	AQUI	AQUAGOLD INTERNATIONAL INC COM	OTC Pink—No Information	Common Stocks
✓	ASCQ	ASCEND ACQUISITION CORP COM NEW	OTCBB—OTCQB	Common Stocks
	ASFJ	ASFG INC COM	Grey Market	Common Stocks
✓	CHFR	CHINA FRUITS CORP COM	OTCQB	Common Stocks
✓	CHOR	CHINA ORGANIC FERTILIZER INC COM	OTC Pink—No Information	Common Stocks
✓	CSNX	CHINA SNX ORGANIC FERTILIZERS COM NEW	Grey Market	Common Stocks
✓	ECGP	ENVIT CAPITAL GROUP INC COM	Grey Market	Common Stocks
	FEKR	FERTIL A CHRON INC COM	Grey Market	Common Stocks
	FEIFF	FORTRESS ENERGY INC COM	Grey Market	Common Stocks
	FIGI	FORTRESS INTL GROUP INC COM	OTCQB	Common Stocks
	FTMK	FORTUNE MARKET MEDIA INC COM NEW	OTC Pink—No Information	Common Stocks

Penny Stocks List

Symbol	Name	Exchange	Security Type
GROT	GROTE MOLEN INC COM	OTCBB—OTCQB	Common Stocks
JMTXF	JAPAN MELTEX INC ORD	Grey Market	Common Stocks
Symbol	Name	Exchange	Security Type
CYCA	CYTTA CORP COM PAR $0.001	OTC Pink—Limited Information	Common Stocks
GSTY	GREEN ST ENERGY INC COM	OTC Pink—No Information	Common Stocks
SAHN	SAUDI AMERICAN HLDGS CORP COM	OTC Pink—No Information	Common Stocks
STOA	SITOA GLOBAL INC COM	OTCQB	Common Stocks
STLM	ST ELMO SILVER MINES CORP COM	OTC Pink—No Information	Common Stocks
SJCH	ST JAMES CAP HLDGS INC COM	Grey Market	Common Stocks
Gbtd	GLOBAL TRIAD INC	Grey Market	
SJKI	ST JOHN KNITS INTL INC COM	OTC Pink—No Information	Common Stocks
CAeo	CHINA RES GROUP LTD		
✓✓✓ STJO	ST JOSEPH INC COM	OTCBB—OTCQB	Common Stocks
EGAN	EGAIN COMMUNICATIONS Corp		
SLAW	ST LAWRENCE ENERGY CORPORATION COM	OTC Pink—No Information	Common Stocks
OARFF	FORT ST JAMES NICKEL CORP COM	Grey Market	Common Stocks
STBMF	ST BARBARA LTD SHS	Grey Market	Common Stocks
SELSF	ST ELIAS LTD COM	Grey Market	Common Stocks
SGKBF	ST GALLER KANTONALBANK REG SHS	Grey Market	Common Stocks
STJPF	ST JAMES S PLACE CAP PLC NEW ORD	OTC Pink—Current	Common Stocks
MDFI	MEDEFILE INTL INC COM	OTCQB	Common Stocks

	MDXX	MEDEX INC NEV COM	OTC Pink—Limited Information	Common Stocks
	BOGMF	BOGO MEDELLIN MLG INC COM	Grey Market	Common Stocks
✓✓✓	AMRI	ALBANY MOLECULAR RESH INC COM	NASDAQ	Common Stocks
	AUNM	AUCTION MILLS INC COM NEW	Grey Market	Common Stocks
✓✓	BAMM	BOOKS-A-MILLION INC COM	NASDAQ	Common Stocks
	BMLS	BURKER MLS INC COM	OTC Pink—No Information	Common Stocks
	CABE	CALIBRE ENERGY INC NEW VOM	OTC Pink—No Information	Common Stocks
	CILZ	CAROLINA MILLS INC COM	OTC Pink—No Information	Common Stocks
	CIMM	CHINA MULTIMEDIA INC COM	Grey Market	Common Stocks
	CWYM	CROWLEY MILNER & COMMON STOCKS COM	Grey Market	Common Stocks
	DBMOF	DEUTSCHE BANK MEXICO SA	Grey Market	Common Stocks
	DFMCF	DIGITAL FUSION MULTIMEDIA CORP COM	OTC Pink—No Information	Common Stocks
	EXTI	EXTENSIONS INC COM	OTC Pink—Limited Information	Common Stocks
	GNTM	GARMAN CABINET & MILLWORK INC COM	OTC Pink—No Information	Common Stocks
✓✓✓	TMGR	GREEN PROCESSING TECH INC COM	OTC Pink—Current Information	Common Stocks
	LWLG	LIGHTWAVE LOGIC INC COM	OTCQB	Common Stocks
✓✓✓	LOJN	LO-JACK CORP COM	NASDAQ	Common Stocks
	LOGC	LOGIC DEVICES INC COM	OTCQX US	Common Stocks
	LOGO	LOGICALOPTIONS INTL INC COM	Grey Market	Common Stocks
	MDLG	MEDIA LOGIC INC COM	Grey Market	Common Stocks
	TPCFF	TITAN LOGIX CORP COM	Grey Market	Common Stocks

Penny Stocks

SCMP	-	SUCampo Pharmaceuticals Inc
PaCEF	-	Pace Oil & Gas LTD—Worth a look
PHLH	-	Pacer Health Corp.com
IPT	-	IPARTY Corp
CYBL	-	Cyberlux Corp
CYTL	-	Cybermesh Corp
CYDI	-	Cybrdi Inc Com
PYMB	-	Pay Mobile Inc
DIGA	-	DIGITAL Angel Corp
LAST	-	Los Angeles SYND Technology
ANGC	-	ANGELES Corp
CSKH	-	Clear Skies Solar Inc
OSTO	-	Original sixteen to one mine com
ZXSI	-	ZAXis Intl Inc
SXNOF	-	SAXON Oil Co
PoL	-	Polo Resources Ltd

Penny Stocks

	Company Symbol		Company Name	Markets
	SHMUF	-	SHIMIZA Corp	Grey Market
	CSTI	-	COSTAR Technologies inc	OTC Pink
	APCN	-	Alliance Pete Core	OTCBB-OTC
✓✓	OREO	-	American Liberty Pete Core	OTCBB-OTCAB
	IGNT	-	INGEN Technologies inc	OTC Pink
✓✓	LFVN	-	Life Vantage Corp	
	FOGC	-	Fortune Oil & Gas inc	OTC Pink
✓✓✓	AXGN	-	AXOGEN INC	OTCQB
✓✓✓	ETEC	-	EMTEC inc	OTCQB
	CNLC	-	China NATL Appliance	OTC Pink
	CRYFQ	-	Crystallex INTL Corp	OTC Pink
✓✓	AWSL	-	Atlantic wind & Solar inc	OTC Pink
	MVIV	-	MViVE inc	Grey Market
	GBVS	-	GLOBAL BEVERAGE Solutions	
✓✓✓	(Unfy) DAEGIS	-	DAEGIS inc	NASDAQ
✓✓✓	FIGI	-	Fortress INTL Group inc	
	MAMS	-	MAM SOFTWARE Group inc	

(SYHO) SYNERGIE WELLNESS PRODUCTS INC—hydrogiene family of personal care systems.

(SMSE) SMS @CTIVE TECHNOLOGIES CORP

(exgp) EXPERTELLIGENCE INC NEW—creating, building and operating Internet businesses.

(AWA) AMERICA WEST HOLDINGS CORP B

RUN—REUNION INDUSTRIES INC

(RAPT) RAPTOR

(JOB) GENERAL EMPLOY ENTPR CORP—Provides staffing services.

ERHC—ERHC ENERGY INC

(agis) AEGIS COMMUNICATIONS GROUP

(nxg) NORTHGATE MINERALS CORP

(MFCO) Microwave Filter Co Inc

(mpet) MAGELLAN PETROLEUM CORP

(omog) OMDA OIL & GAS INC

(actt) ACT TELECONFERENCING INC—provides audio, video, and data

(mspd) MINDSPEED TECHNOLOGIES IN

(Rmkr) RAINMAKER SYSTEMS INC—Internet-enabling and marketing services.

(CICI) COMMUNICATION INTELLIGENCE CO

(FONR) FONAR CORP—manufactures magnetic resonance imaging {MRI} scanners.

(Axgi) ARCHIPELAGO HOLDINGS, INC

Penny Stocks

Symbol	Name	Exchange	Security Type
GIMU	GLOBAL IMMUNE TECH INC COM	OTC Pink—Limited Information	Common Stocks
IMNG	IMING CORP COM	OTC Pink—Limited Information	Common Stocks
IMMFF	IMMUNE NETWORK LTD COM NEW	OTC Pink—No Information	Common Stocks
IMUT	IMMUNETREE INTL INC COM	OTC Pink—No Information	Common Stocks
IMBI	IMMUNOBIOTICS INC COM	OTC Pink—No Information	Common Stocks
✓IMUC	IMMUNOCELLULAR THERAPEUTICS COM	NYSE MKT LLC	Common Stocks
✓IMGN	IMMUNOGEN INC COM	OTC Pink	Common Stocks
✓✓IMMU	IMMUNOMEDICS INC COM	NASDAQ	Common Stocks
IMYN	IMMUNOSYN CORP COM	OTC Pink—No Information	Common Stocks
IMMB	IMMUNOTECH LABORATORIES INC COM	OTC Pink—Limited	Common Stocks
IMUN	IMMUNOVATIVE INC COM	OTCQB	Common Stocks
IMMVF	IMMUNO VACCINE INC COM	Grey Market	Common Stocks
IMMNF	IMMUNODIAGNOSTIC SYS HLDG PLC SHS	Grey Market	Common Stocks
IMMTF	IMMUNOTEC INC COM	Grey Market	Common Stocks
✓FTER	FORTERUS INC COM	OTC Pink—No Information	Common Stocks
✓FORBQ	FORTICELL BIOSCIENCE INC COM	OTC Pink—No Information	Common Stocks
BBVVF	BBV VIETNAM S E A ACQ CORP BR SHS	OTC Pink—No Information	Common Stocks
BGMO	BERGAMO ACQUISITION CORP COM	OTC Pink—Limited Information	Common Stocks
CVHPF	CHINA VANTAGEPOINT ACQUISITION SHS	OTCBB—OTCQB	Common Stocks
CCAJ	COASTAL CAP ACQUISITION CORP COM	OTC Pink—Current Information	Common Stocks
CCAC	COMMITTED CAP ACQUISITION CORP COM	OTCQB	Common Stocks

Penny Stocks Symbols

LOMT✓	ADHC	USBF
WGas	PZOO	PRTN
Sndy	NAGP	SAPX
ALZM	MIBI	LDPP
RTGV	TFIV✓	RVNG
BBDA	CFGA✓	HAIR
CCAJ	EMWW✓	NAGP
PCFG	ECTH✓✓	FRCN
SGGH✓	WTWO	LBGO
FRCN	LYJN	ADLI
AMWI	CPMCF	ALCD
LOMT	NSRS	ALISO
SNDY	LEXG	ESCD
FRCN	PEIX	DLTA
SNDY	WGAS	AVIC
BBDA	RTGV	CCAJ
	HERO	SGGH
		ALZM
		AMWI

NYSE & NASDAQ under $5 Stocks

CBAK	-	CHINA BAK BATTERY INC
CCCL	-	CHINA CERAMICS CO
CHYR	-	CHRYON CORP
DRL	-	DORAL FINL CORP
ANTP	-	PHAZAR CORP
✓✓ GST	-	GASTAR EXPL LTD
BRD	-	BRIGUS GOLD CORP
✓ KFS	-	KINGWAY FINL SVCS INC
✓ CTC	-	IFM INVTS LTD
✓ DSTI	-	DAYSTAR TECHNOLOGIES INC
✓ DL	-	CHINA DISTANCE ED HLDGS LTD
CFBK	-	CENTRAL FED CORP
✓ CHCI	-	COMSTOCK HLDG COS INC
✓ CHTP	-	CHELSEA THERAPEUTICS INTL LTD
✓ CHLN	-	CHINA HOUSING & LAND DEV INC
✓ CGR	-	CLAUDE RES INC
SHZ	-	CHINA SHEN ZHOU MNG & RES INC
API	-	ADVANCED PHOTONIX INC
✓ CAK	-	CAMAC ENERGY INC
✓ CEP	-	CONSTELLATION ENERGY PRTNR
CMFO	-	CHINA MARINE FOOD GROUP LTD
CRC	-	CHROMCRAFT REVINGTON INC

NYSE & NASDAQ under 5$ stocks

✓ CRV	-	COAST DISTR SYS
CUR	-	NEURALSTEM INC
CXZ	-	CROSSHAIR ENERGY CORP
DPW	-	DIGITAL PWR CORP
✓ DNN	-	DENISON MINES CORP
EGI	-	ENTREE GOLD INC
ERB	-	ERBA DIAGNOSTICS
ESA	-	ENERGY SVCS OF AMERICA CORP
ETAK	-	ELEPHANT TALK COMM CORP
EVI	-	ENVIROSTAR INC
EVK	-	EVER GLORY INTL
✓ GGR	-	GEOGLOBAL RESOURCES INC = oil search in Barbados & Israel very cheap stocks take a look
GIG	-	GIGTIX INC
✓ ITI	-	ITERIS INC—worth taking a look
KGN	-	KEEGAN RES INC
LON	-	LONCOR RESOURCES INC
✓ LTS	-	LADENBURG THALMAN—worth taking a look
MCZ	-	MAD CATZ INTERATIVE INC
MGH	-	MINCO GOLD CORP
✓MOC	-	COMMAND SEC CORP—worth taking a look
NBS	-	NEOSTEM INC
NEWN	-	NEW ENERGY GROUP

NYSE & NASDAQ stocks under 5$

ABTL   -   AUTOBY TEL INC
VSR   -   VERSAR INC—Future look good a must look
ALIM   -   ALIMERA SCIENCES INC
ALRN   -   AMERICAN LEARNING CORP
WEX   -   WINLAND ELECTRS INC
ABIO   -   ARCA BIOPHARMA INC
ALTI   -   ALTAIR NANOTECHNOLOGIES INC
WGA   -   WELLS GARDNER ELECTRS CORPS
ABCD   -   CAMBIUM LEARNING GRP INC
WRN   -   WESTERN COPPER & GOLD CORP
AAME   -   ATLANTIC AMERN CORP
WYY   -   WIDEPOINT CORP—worth a look
ZBB   -   ZBB ENERGY CORP—A must look
XPL   -   SOLITARIO EXPL & RTY CORP
ALVR   -   ALVARION LTD
AMCF   -   ANDATEE CHINA MARINE FUEL SVCS
AMCN   -   AIRMEDIA GROUP INC
ASTM   -   AASTROM BIOSCIENCES INC
AMRI   -   ALBANY MOLECULAR RESH INC
ARQL   -   ARQULE INC
APWC   -   ASIA PACIFIC WIRE & CABLE CORP
TAT   -   TRANSATLANTIC PETROLEUM LTD
TCX   -   TUCOWS INC
TGB   -   TASEKO MINES LTD
THM   -   INTERNATIONAL TOWER HILL MINES
TLR   -   TIMBERLINE RES CORP
TOF   -   TOFUTTI BRANDS INC
TRT   -   TRIO TECH INTL
UAMY   -   UNITED STATES ANTIMONY CORP
UEC   -   URANIUM ENERGY CORP
UQM   -   UQM TECHNOLOGIES INC
URZ   -   URANERZ ENERGY CORP
ACTS   -   ACTIONS SEMICONDUCTOR CO
ACRX   -   ACELRX PHARMACEUTICAL INC—worth looking
ATHX   -   ATHERSYS INC
UVE   -   UNIVERSAL INS HLDGS INC
ACLS   -   AXCELIS TECHNOLOGIES INC—worth looking
VGZ   -   VISTA GOLD
ACFC   -   ATLANTIC COAST FINL CORP
ADAT   -   AUTHENTIDATE HLDG CORP

ACAD	-	ACADIA PHARMACEUTICALS INC—Take a look
AHPI	-	ALLIED HEALTH CARE PRODS INC
NTN	-	BUZZTIME INC—worth taking a look
OBT	-	ORBITAL CORP
ONP	-	ORIENT PAPER INC—pays dividents
PAL	-	NORTH AMERN PALLADIUM LTD
PCYG	-	PARK CITY GROUP INC
PIP	-	PHARMATHENE INC
PZG	-	PARAMOUNT GOLD & SILVER CORP
QRM	-	QUEST RARE MINERALS LTD
RLGT	-	RADIANT LOGISTICS—Worth taking a look
ROX	-	CASTLE BRANDS INC—Worth taking a look
RTK	-	RENTECH INC
RVP	-	RETRACTABLE TECHNOLOGIES INC
RWC	-	RELM WIRELESS CORP
SED	-	SED INTL HLDGS INC
SNT	-	SENESCO TECHNOLOGIES INC—very cheap stocks, take a look
SOQ	-	SONDERES CORP—Oil & Gas operations
SSY	-	SUNLINK HEALTH SYSTEMS INC
STS	-	SUPREME INDS INC
SYN	-	SYNTHETIC BIOLOGICS INC
TAS	-	TASMAN METAL LTD
APRI	-	APRICUS BIOSCIENCES INC
AMRS	-	AMYRIS INC
AMSC	-	AMERICAN SUPERCONDUCTOR CORP
APPY	-	ASPENBIO PHARMA INC
ANTH	-	ANTHERA PHARMACEUTICALS INC *worth a look*
ANCI	-	AMERICAN CARESOURCE HLDGS INC
ANAD	-	ANADIGICS INC

Companies that worth a look

✓ Lullemon   - Lulu
CNX   - Con
Al Coa   - AA
Smith & Wesson   - SWNC
Broadwind Energy Inc   - Bwen
✓ Buffalo wings   - Bwld
Target   - T.GT
Aecom Technology Corp - ACM
✓ Expedia Inc   - Expe
First Solar   - FSLR
✓ Franklin Covey Co   - FC

Oil & Gas Stocks

TIDE	-	TIDELANDS Oil & Gas Corp—Penny Stock
TLM	-	TALISMAN ENERGY Inc—Pays Divident
AE	-	ADAMS RES & ENERGY Inc.—Pays Divident
MMR	-	MCMORAN EXPLORATION Co
CPE	-	CALLON PETE Co—A stocks to look at
GTY	-	GETTY RLTY Corp—Pays Divident
GDP	-	GOODRICH PETE Corp
SSL	-	SASOL LTD Sponsored—Pays Divident
DBLE	-	DOUBLE EAGLE PETE Co—cheap stocks take a look
RRC	-	RANGE RES Corp
AHC	-	AH BELO Corp—Pay Divident, take a look
APU	-	AMERIGAS PARTNERS LP—Pay Divident—take a look
BPT	-	BP PRUDHOE Bay Pay High Divident—A must look ✓
LNGYF	-	LNG ENERGY LTD—A penny stocks
LNG	-	CHENIERE ENERGY INC—Future looks promising
EPD	-	ENTERPRISE PRODS PARTNERS—Pays Divident ✓
FGP	-	FERRELL GAS PARTNERS—Pays Divident ✓
MWE	-	MARKWEST PARTNERS—Pays Divident ✓

Symbol		*Oil Stocks*	*? aprox Annual Dividents*
CNQ	-	Canadian Natural Resources Ltd-------------- Oil & Gas - 0.29	
COP	-	Conoco Philips ------------------------------------ Oil & Gas - 2.15	
CEO	-	Cnooc Ltd -- Oil & Gas - 5.28	
CVX	-	Chevron Corp------------------------------------- Oil & Gas - 2.84	
NE	-	Noble Corp-------------------------------------- Oil & Gas - 0 79	
OXY	-	Occidental Petroleum ------------------------ Oil & Gas - 1.47	
Nsh	-	Nustar GP Holding LLC---------------------- Oil & Gas - 1.39	
RDS-A	-	Royal Dutch Shell PLC-A--------------------- Oil & Gas - 3.36	
XOM	-	Exon Mobil Corp -------------------------------- Oil & Gas - 1.74	
SU	-	Suncor Energy Inc -----------------------------Oil & Gas - 0 38¢	
iMO	-	Imperial Oil Ltd --------------------------------Oil & Gas - 0 42¢	
WMB	-	Williams Companies---------------------------Oil & Gas - 0 49¢	
EnB	-	Enbridge Inc------------------------------------- Oil & Gas - 1.65	
HP	-	Helmerich and Payne Inc --------------------- Oil & Gas - 0 22	

Symbol		Quality Oil and Energy Stocks
HES	-	HESS
CVX	-	CHEVRON Corp
COP	-	CONOCO Phillips
EC	-	ECCPETRCL SA
TOT	-	TOTAL SA
RDSB	-	ROYAL DUTCH SHELL PLC
XOM	-	EXXON Mobil Corp
CQP	-	CHENIERE ENERGY PARTNERS
REP	-	REP SOIL ASA
LNG	-	Cheniere Energy Inc
STO	-	STATOIL ASA Sponsored
VLO	-	VALERO ENERGY
OXY	-	Occidental Petroleum Corp
CNX	-	CONSOL ENERGY Inc
PTR	-	PETROChina Co Ltd

America Sweet Heart Stocks

Symbol Company name

Symbol		Company name
Cost	-	Costco wholesale
Pep	-	Pepsi
UPS	-	UPS
XOM	-	EXXON Mobile
TXN	-	Texas instrument
Dis	-	Walt des
TWX	-	Time Warner
HRB	-	H & R Block
ORCL	-	oricle
KMB	-	Kimblelee Clark
CBS	-	CBC
VZ	-	Verizion
AXP	-	America Express
DD	-	DuPoint
Gis	-	Genal Mills
J&J	-	Johnson & Johnson
Pep	-	Pepsico
T	-	AT & T
ViA	-	Via Com
BXP	-	Boston Propert
HG	-	
LMCA	-	Liberty Media Corp
DG	-	dollar general
MRK	-	Merch
ARun	-	Aruba networks
Kmb	-	Kimberly Clark

Met	-	Met Life
TsCo	-	Tractor Supply
STJ	-	St Jude Medical
JPM	-	JP Morgan Chase
Tol	-	Toll Brothers
CVX	-	
AAPL	-	Apple
HRB	-	H&R Block
Expe	-	Expidetor
BBBY	-	Bed Bath be
AMZN	-	Amazon
INCT	-	intel
F	-	Ford
IBM	-	IBM
CSCo	-	Cisco system
LNG	-	
DLTR	-	dollar tree
LLY	-	Eli Lilly

Quality Stocks

FDX	-	FedX
GS	-	Goldman Sachs
BIDV	-	Baidu
PCCN	-	price line
BA	-	Boeing
CL	-	Colgate Palmolive
GooG	-	Google
HD	-	Home depo
Ko	-	Cocoa Cola
NKE	-	Nike
PG	-	Proter Gamble
Pru	-	Prudential
WFC	-	Well Forgo
WMT	-	Walmart

Quality Stocks

Symbol Company name

LuLu	-	Lululermon
DE	-	Deer
FDX	-	Fedex
PCLn	-	priceline.com
GooG	-	Google
Txn	-	Texas instruments
EXPE	-	Expedia
BAC	-	Bank of America
AAPL	-	Apple
CSCO	-	Cisco
HES	-	Hess
AMZN	-	Amazon
KO	-	Coca Cola
CSC	-	Computer Science
Pot	-	Direct rise
Azo	-	Auto Zone
INTC	-	Intel
GS	-	Goldman Sach
EBAY	-	Ebay
VIAB	-	Via Com
ED	-	Conedison
CAT	-	Caterpillar
APOL	-	Apollogro
ACAS	-	American Capital Ltd
ACI	-	Arch Coal Inc
ADM	-	Archer-Daniels-Midland Co
ADSK	-	Autodesk Inc
AGO	-	Assured Guaranty Ltd
ANR	-	Alpha Natural Resources Inc
APA	-	Apache Corp
APWR	-	A-Power Energy Generation Systems Ltd
ATPG	-	ATP Oil & Gas Corp/United States
BAX	-	Baxter International Inc
BBBY	-	Bed Bath & Beyond Inc
BHI	-	Baker Hughes Inc
BPOP	-	Popular Inc
AGNC	-	American Capital Agency Corp
LULU	-	Lululermon Athletica Inc

SINA	-	Sina Corp
FFIV	-	FS Networks
GM	-	General Motors Company
MPC	-	Moly Corp Inc
RVBD	-	Riverbed Technology Inc
Bidu	-	Baidu
WIN	-	Windstream Corp
WMB	-	Williams Cos Inc/The
XLK	-	Technology Select Sector SPDR Fund
XLP	-	Consumer Staples Select Sector SPDR Fund
XLV	-	Health Care Select Sector SPDR Fund
XLY	-	Consumer Discretionary Sel. Sec. SPDR Fund
XME	-	SPDR S&P Metals & Mining ETF
GE	-	General Electric Company
EWJ	-	iShares MSCI Japan Index Fund
FDX	-	FedEx Corp
FNM	-	Federal National Mortgage Association
FRE	-	Federal Home Loan Mortgage Corp
GILD	-	Gilead Sciences Inc
GLW	-	Corning Inc
HBC	-	HSBC Holdings PLC
HES	-	Hess Corp
HL	-	Hecla Mining Co
HOG	-	Harley-Davidson Inc
HON	-	Honeywell International Inc
JOYG	-	Joy Global Inc
JWN	-	Nordstrom Inc
KFT	-	Kraft Foods Inc
LEAP	-	Leap Wireless International Inc
LLY	-	Eli Lilly & Co
LO	-	Lorillard Inc
LOW	-	Lowe's Cos Inc
M	-	Macy's Inc
MCO	-	Moody's Corp
MET	-	MetLife Inc
MMM	-	3M Co
MU	-	Micron Technology Inc
NUE	-	Nucor Corp
OXY	-	Occidental Petroleum Corp
PARD	-	Poniard Pharmaceuticals Inc
PEP	-	PepsiCo Inc/NC
PM	-	Philip Morris International Inc

PNC	-	PNC Financial Services Group Inc
QID	-	ProShares UltraShort QQQ
SHLD	-	Sears Holdings Corp
SLM	-	SLM Corp
SLW	-	Silver Wheaton Corp
SQNM	-	Sequenom Inc
STEC	-	STEC Inc
STX	-	Seagate Technology
ACL	-	Alcon Inc
ADBE	-	Adobe Systems Inc
AKS	-	AK Steel Holding Corp
ALL	-	Allstate Corp/The
AMED	-	Amedisys Inc
AMLN	-	Amylin Pharmaceuticals Inc
APOL	-	Apollo Group Inc
BHP	-	BHP Billiton Ltd
BRKB	-	Berkshire Hathaway Inc
BSX	-	Boston Scientific Corp
BUCY	-	Bucyrus International Inc
CELG	-	Celgene Corp
CENX	-	Century Aluminum Co
CIEN	-	Ciena Corp
CLF	-	Cliffs Natural Resources Inc
COST	-	Costco Wholesale Corp
CREE	-	Cree Inc
CTIC	-	Cell Therapeutics Inc
DAL	-	Delta Air Lines Inc
DHI	-	DR Horton Inc
DTV	-	DIRECTV
DVN	-	Devon Energy Corp
ENER	-	Energy Conversion Devices Inc
EP	-	El Paso Corp
EWT	-	iShares MSCI Taiwan Index Fund
FXE	-	CurrencyShares Euro Trust
GFI	-	Gold Fields Ltd
GMCR	-	Green Mountain Coffee Roasters Inc
GME	-	GameStop Corp
GRMN	-	Garmin Ltd
HK	-	Petrohawk Energy Corp
CB	-	Chubb Corp
CI	-	CIGNA Corp
CL	-	Colgate-Palmolive Co

CMA	-	Comerica Inc
CNX	-	Consol Energy Inc
CRM	-	Salesforce.com Inc
DCTH	-	Delcath Systems Inc
DO	-	Diamond Offshore Drilling Inc
EK	-	Eastman Kodak Co
EOG	-	EOG Resources Inc
ESI	-	ITT Educational Services Inc
ESRX	-	Express Scripts Inc
EWW	-	iShares MSCI Mexico Investable Market Index
BAC	-	Bank of America Corporation BAC
DELL	-	Dell, Inc.
EBAY	-	eBay, Inc.
EEM	-	iShares MSCI Emerging Mkts. Index Fund
EMC	-	EMC Corporation
F	-	Ford Motor Company
GS	-	Goldman Sachs Group, Inc
HAL	-	Halliburton Company
HD	-	The Home Depot, Inc.
JPM	-	JPMorgan Chase & Co.
MNX	-	Mini-NASDAQ OMX Index
NEM	-	Newmont Mining Corporation
PFE	-	Pfizer, Inc.
SBUX	-	Starbucks Corporation
SNDK	-	SanDisk Corporation
TGT	-	Target Corporation
VALE	-	Vale SA
VLO	-	Valero Energy Corporation
VZ	-	Verizon Communications, Inc.
WMT	-	Walmart Stores, Inc.
XOM	-	Exxon Mobil Corporation
SU	-	Suncor Energy Inc
TCK	-	Teck Resources Ltd
TEVA	-	Teva Pharmaceutical Industries Ltd
TLT	-	iShares Barclays 20+ Year Treasury Bond Fund
TZA	-	Direxion Daily Small Cap Bear 3x Shares
UAUA	-	UAL Corp
URE	-	ProShares Ultra Real Estate
UTX	-	United Technologies Corp
WFR	-	MEMC Electronic Materials Inc
WFT	-	Weatherford International Ltd
WLP	-	WellPoint Inc

XLB	-	Materials Select Sector SPDR Fund
XRX	-	Xerox Corp
XTO	-	XTO Energy Inc
YRCW	-	YRC Worldwide Inc

Fund

EWY	-	iShares MSCI South Korea Index Fund
FIS	-	Fidelity National Information Services Inc
FWLT	-	Foster Wheeler AG
FXP	-	ProShares UltraShort FTSE/Xinhua China 25
GENZ	-	Genzyme Corp
GGP	-	General Growth Properties Inc
GIS	-	General Mills Inc
GPS	-	Gap Inc/The
HBAN	-	Huntington Bancshares Inc/OH
HOT	-	Starwood Hotels & Resorts Worldwide Inc
HSY	-	Hershey Co/The
IBN	-	ICICI Bank Ltd
JDSU	-	JDS Uniphase Corp
KEY	-	KeyCorp
KMP	-	Kinder Morgan Energy Partners LP
KRE	-	SPDR KBW Regional Banking ETF
LNC	-	Lincoln National Corp
MA	-	Mastercard Inc
MBI	-	MBIA Inc
MRO	-	Marathon Oil Corp
MTG	-	MGIC Investment Corp
MYL	-	Mylan Inc/PA
AA		
AIG	-	American International Group, Inc.
COF	-	Capital One Financial Corp
CVX	-	Chevron Corp
DE	-	Deere & Co
DOW	-	Dow Chemical Co/The
DRYS	-	DryShips Inc
EFA	-	iShares MSCI EAFE Index Fund
ETFC	-	E*Trade Financial Corp
EWZ	-	iShares MSCI Brazil Index Fund
FAS	-	Direxion Daily Financial Bull 3X Shares
FAZ	-	Direxion Daily Financial Bear 3X Shares

FITB	-	Fifth Third Bancorp
FSLR	-	First Solar Inc
FXI	-	iShares FTSE/Xinhua China 25 Index Fund
GDX	-	Market Vectors—Gold Miners ETF
GG	-	Goldcorp Inc
GLD	-	SPDR Gold Trust
HGSI	-	Human Genome Sciences Inc
HIG	-	Hartford Financial Services Group Inc
HPQ	-	Hewlett-Packard Co
IBM	-	International Business Machines Corp
IYR	-	iShares Dow Jones US Real Estate Index Fund
JNJ	-	Johnson & Johnson
JNPR	-	Juniper Networks Inc
KO	-	Coca-Cola Co/The
LVS	-	Las Vegas Sands Corp
MCD	-	McDonald's Corp
MGM	-	MGM Mirage
MON	-	Monsanto Co
MOS	-	Mosaic Co/The
MRK	-	Merck & Co Inc/NJ
MS	-	Morgan Stanley
NLY	-	Annaly Capital Management Inc
NOK	-	Nokia OYJ
NVDA	-	Nvidia Corp
ORCL	-	Oracle Corp
PALM	-	Palm Inc
BIDU	-	Baidu Inc/China

Microsystems, Inc.

ABK	-	Ambac Financial Group, Inc.

Energy Inc.

NBR	-	Nabors Industries Ltd
NE	-	Noble Corp
NKE	-	NIKE Inc
NOV	-	National Oilwell Varco Inc
NTAP	-	NetApp Inc
PCL	-	Plum Creek Timber Co Inc

PHM	-	Pulte Group Inc
PXP	-	Plains Exploration & Production Co
QLD	-	ProShares Ultra QQQ
RCL	-	Royal Caribbean Cruises Ltd
RSH	-	RadioShack Corp
SO	-	Southern Co
SUN	-	Sunoco Inc
SWN	-	Southwestern Energy Co
TSL	-	Trina Solar Ltd
TSO	-	Tesoro Corp
TWX	-	Time Warner Inc
TXT	-	Textron Inc
TYC	-	Tyco International Ltd
VRSN	-	VeriSign Inc
VVUS	-	Vivus Inc
WHR	-	Whirlpool Corp
WLT	-	Walter Energy Inc
XL	-	XL Group Plc
XLNX	-	Xilinx Inc
XOP	-	SPDR S&P Oil & Gas Exploration & Production ETF
YUM	-	Yum! Brands Inc
IWM	-	Ishares Russell 2000
CAT	-	Caterpillar Inc.
QQQQ	-	NASDAQ 100 Tracking Index
SMH	-	Semiconductor Holders
TXN	-	Texas Instruments Inc.
A	-	Agilent Technologies Inc.
AMD	-	Advanced Micro Devices
FLEX	-	Flextronics International
ABT	-	Abbott Laboratories
AEM	-	Agnico-Eagle Mines, Ltd
AET	-	Aetna Inc
AFL	-	Aflac Inc
AKAM	-	Akamai Technologies Inc
AMAT	-	Applied Materials Inc
AMR	-	AMR Corp
ANF	-	Abercrombie & Fitch Co
APC	-	Anadarko Petroleum Corp
ATVI	-	Activision Blizzard Inc
BBD	-	Banco Bradesco SA
BCRX	-	BioCryst Pharmaceuticals Inc.
BK	-	Bank of New York Mellon Corp./The

BRCM	-	Broadcom Crop
BTU	-	Peabody Energy Corp
BX	-	Blackstone Group LP
CAL	-	Continental Airlines Inc
CF	-	CF Industries Holdings Inc
CMCSA	-	Comcast Corp
CSX	-	CSX Corp
CVS	-	CVS Caremark Corp
CX	-	Cemex SAB de CV
DD	-	El du Pont de Nemours & Co
ERTS	-	Electronic Arts Inc
MOT	-	Motorola, Inc.
NYX	-	NYSE Euronext
OIH	-	Oil Services HLDRS
QCOM	-	Qualcomm, Inc.
RIMM	-	Research in Motion Ltd.
SPY	-	SPDR S&P 500
T	-	AT&T, Inc.
XLE	-	Energy Select Sector SPDR
XLF	-	Financial Select Sector SPDR
YHOO	-	Yahoo!. Inc.
AAPL	-	Apple, Inc.
AMGN	-	Amgen, Inc.
AMZN	-	Amazon.com, Inc.
BMY	-	Bristol-Myers Squibb Co.
C	-	Citigroup, Inc.
COP	-	ConocoPhillips
CSCO	-	Cisco Systems
DIA	-	Diamonds Trust
DNDN	-	Dendreon Corp.
FCX	-	Freeport-McMoRan Copper & Gold, Inc.
MO	-	Altria Group, Inc.
PBR	-	Petroleo Brasileiro SA
PG	-	Procter & Gamble Co/The
POT	-	Potash Corp of Saskatchewan Inc
RF	-	Regions Financial Corp
RIG	-	Transocean Ltd
RMBS	-	Rambus Inc
S	-	Sprint Nextel Corp
SDS	-	ProShares UltraShort S&P500
SKF	-	ProShares UltraShort Financials
SLB	-	Schlumberger Ltd

SLV	-	iShares Silver Trust
SRS	-	ProShares UltraShort Real Estate
SSO	-	ProShares Ultra S&P500
STI	-	SunTrust Banks Inc
SVNT	-	Savient Pharmaceuticals Inc
TBT	-	ProShares UltraShort 20+ Year Treasury
UNG	-	United States Natural Gas Fund LP
UNH	-	UnitedHealth Group Inc
UPS	-	United Parcel Service Inc
USB	-	US Bancorp
USO	-	United States Oil Fund LP
UYG	-	ProShares Ultra Financials
V	-	Visa Inc
WFC	-	Wells Fargo & Co
WYNN	-	Wynn Resorts Ltd
X	-	United States Steel Corp
XHB	-	SPDR S&P Homebuilders ETF
XLI	-	Industrial Select Sector SPDR Fund
XLU	-	Utilities Select Sector SPDR Fund
BRCD	-	Brocade
DIS	-	The Walt Disney Company
GNW	-	Genworth Financial Inc.
UUP	-	Powershares DB US Dollar Index Bullish Fund
IOC	-	InterOil Corp
IP	-	International Paper Co
ITMN	-	InterMune Inc
JCP	-	JC Penney Co Inc
KBH	-	KB Home
KGC	-	Kinross Gold Corp
LCC	-	US Airways Group Inc
LDK	-	LDK Solar Co Ltd
LEN	-	Lennar Corp
MDT	-	Medtronic Inc
MDVN	-	Medivation Inc
MEE	-	Massey Energy Co
MJN	-	Mead Johnson Nutrition Co
MMR	-	McMoRan Exploration Co
MNKD	-	MannKind Corp
MRVL	-	Marvell Technology Group Ltd
MT	-	ArcelorMittal
NFLX	-	NetFlix Inc
PCX	-	Patriot Coal Corp

PRU	-	Prudential Financial Inc
RTN	-	Raytheon Co
SEED	-	Origin Agritech Ltd
SII	-	Smith International Inc
SIRI	-	Sirius XM Radio Inc
SPG	-	Simon Property Group Inc
SPWRA	-	SunPower Corp
STP	-	Suntech Power Holdings Co Ltd
STT	-	State Street Corp
SYMC	-	Symantec Corp
TIF	-	Tiffany & Co
TIVO	-	TiVo Inc
TLB	-	Talbots Inc
TM	-	Toyota Motor Corp
UNP	-	Union Pacific Corp
WAG	-	Walgreen Co
WDC	-	Western Digital Corp

Dividend Stocks

—Distributions of a company's profit, paid out to common and preferred shareholders. Usually dividends are paid out on a quarterly basis in the form of a cash dividend, as determined by a company's board of directors.

—Information on some of these companies are not available.

- **ASB financial corp (Asbp)**
- ASBP is a unitary savings and loan holding company for American Savings Bank, FSB, a federal savings bank.

- **Acme united corp (Acu)**
- ACU produces scissors, shears, rulers, first aid kits and related products, which are sold to wholesale, contract and retail stationary distributors, office supply stores, retailers and mass market retailers.

- **Albemarle Corp (Alb)**
- Albemarle Corp. is a major producer of specialty polymers & fine chemicals, including polymer intermediates, cleaning product intermediates & additives, agrichemical intermediates, pharmachemical intermediates & bulk actives, catalysts & brominated flame retardants.

- **BB&T corp (bbt)**
- BB&T is a multi-bank holding Co. that conducts its operations in NC, SC, VA, MD, GA, WV, KY & Washington D.C.

Allway Check Annual Dividend and Annual Yield because it some times changes. (Don't forget)

Good Yield Divident Stocks

Symbol	Company name
CSCO	Cisco Systems
CZNC	Citizens & Northern
CHCO	City Holding
CNL	Cleco
CKSW	ClickSoftware Technologies
CLF	Cliffs Natural Resources
CME	CME Group
CMS	CMS Energy
CCNE	CNB Financial
CLP	Colonial Properties Trust
CLNY	Colony Financial
CMC	Commercial Metals
CWH	CommonWealth REIT
JCS	Communications Systems
CBU	Community Bank System
CTBI	Community Trust Bancorp
CODI	Compass Diversified Holdings
CMP	Compass Minerals International
GSJK	Compressco Partners
CPSI	Computer Programs & Systems
CIX	CompX International
CMTL	Comtech Telecomm.
CAG	ConAgra Foods
CCUR	Concurrent Computer
CTWS	Connecticut Water Service
COP	ConocoPhillips
CNSL	Consolidated Communications Holdings
CWCO	Consolidated Water
CPNO	Copano Energy, L.L.C.
COR	CoreSite Realty
CFP	Cornerstone Progressive Return Fund
GLW	Corning
OFC	Corporate Office Properties Trust

CJREF	Corus Entertainment
CMRE	Costamare
CRRC	Courier
CVA	Covanta Holding
CBRL	Cracker Barrel Old Country Store
CR	Crane
CRD.B	Crawford
F.T.R.	Frontier Communication
PG	Procter & Gamble
M.C.D.	McDonald
HSY	Hershey Co
KMB	Kimberly Clark Corp
K	Kellogg Co
HUM	Humana Inc
MMM	3M Co
UTX	United Technologies Corp
T	AT&T INC
VZ	Verizon Communications Inc
DE	Deere & Co
IBM	International Business Machs
VIA	VIA Com Inc
WMT	WAL-MART Stores Inc
KO	Coca Cola Co
PEP	PEPSICO Inc
UNH	United Health Group Inc
BA	Boeing Co
SLB	Schlumberger Ltd
UNP	Union Pac Corp
CQP	Cheniere Energy Partners
VLO	Valero Energy Corp
TOT	Total SA Sponsored ADR
STO	STAT OIL ASA Sponsored ADR
WY	Weyerhaeuser Co
MUR	Murphy Oil Corp
WYNN	Resorts Ltd
ACN	Accenture PLC Ireland
ETR	Entergy Corp

PSA	Public Storage
BXP	Boston Properties
LECO	Lincoln Elec Hldgs
NEE	Nextera Energy Inc
NEE PR.H	Nextera Energy CAP
MPC	Marathon Corp
BTU	Peabody Energy Corp
TOT:	Total SA Sponsored
HD	Home Depot Inc
PPL	PPL Corp
RL	Ralph lauren Corp
TYC	Tyco International Ltd
UPS	United Parcel Service Inc
HON	Honeywell Intl Inc
CL	Colgate Palmolive Co
ABT	Abbott Labs
AFL	AFLAC Inc
LLY	Lilly Eli & Co
DD	Duponteide Nemours
BOE	Blackrock Global
D	Dominion Inc
DOW	DOW Chem Co
DRI	Darden Restaurants Inc
PG	Procter & Gamble Co
LVS	Las Vegas Sands
GD	General Dynamics Corp
SHLM	A. Schulman
ABT	Abbott Laboratories
ABM	ABM Industries
AKR	Acadia Realty Trust
ACMP	Access Midstream Partners
ACE	ACE Limited
ACU	Acme United
AVCA	Advocat
AFL	AFLAC
MITT	AG Mortgage Investment Trust
GAS	AGL Resources
ADC	Agree Realty

APD	Air Products & Chemicals
AYR	Aircastle Limited
AIN	Albany International
ARE	Alexandria Real Estate Equities
ALE	ALLETE
ALNC	Alliance Financial
AHGP	Alliance Holdings GP
ARLP	Alliance Resource Partners
AB	AllianceBernstein Holding
LNT	Alliant Energy
MO	Altria Group
EPAX	Ambassadors Group
ACO	AMCOL International
AEE	Ameren
AAT	American Assets Trust
ACC	American Campus Communities
AGNC	American Capital Agency
MTGE	American Capital Mortgage Investment
AEP	American Electric Power
AM	American Greetings
AMID	American Midstream Partners
AMNB	American National BankShares
ARCT	American Realty Capital Trust
ASEI	American Science & Engineering
AMSWA	American Software
AWR	American States Water
AWK	American Water Works
APU	AmeriGas Partners
AMP	Ameriprise Financial
ASCA	Ameristar Casinos
ADI	Analog Devices
NLY	Annaly Capital Management
ANH	Anworth Mortgage Asset
AIV	Apartment Investment and Management
ARI	Apollo Commercial Real Est. Finance
AINV	Apollo Investment
AMTG	Apollo Residential Mortgage
AMAT	Applied Materials

WTR	Aqua America
ARCC	Ares Capital
AI	Arlington Asset Investment
ARR	ARMOUR Residential REIT
AROW	Arrow Financial
ARTNA	Artesian Resources
AJG	Arthur J. Gallagher
AHT	Ashford Hospitality Trust
ALC	Assisted Living Concepts
AEC	Associated Estates Realty
AGO	Assured Guaranty
T	AT&T
ATLS	Atlas Energy
APL	Atlas Pipeline Partners
TWX	Time Warner Inc
PRU	Prudential Finl Inc
YUM	Brands Inc
WM	Waste Mgmt Inc
WHR	WhirlPool Corp
CLX	Clorox Co
SUN	Sunolo Inc
DTE	DTE Energy Co
DUK	Duke Energy Corp
EE	Elpaso Elec Co
APL	Atlas Pipeline Partners
EDWES	Consolidated Edison Inc
NS	Nustar Energy
CPNO	Copano Energy
MWE	Markwest Energy
EMR	Emerson Elec Co
CQP	Cheniere Energy Partners
ADP	Automatic Data Processing
AVB	AvalonBay Communities
AVY	Avery Dennison
AVA	Avista
AVP	Avon Products
AVX	AVX Corporation
AXS	Axis Capital Holdings Limited

BGS	B&G Foods
BWINB	Baldwin & Lyons
BANF	BancFirst
BLX	Banco Latioamericano Comerc Exterior
BOCH	Bank of Commerce Holdings
BOH	Bank of Hawaii
BMO	Bank of Montreal
BNS	Bank of Nova Scotia
BKU	BankUnited
BHB	Bar Harbor Bankshares
BAX	Baxter International
BTE	Baytex Energy
BBT	BB&T
BCE	BCE
BLC	Belo
BMS	Bemis
BHLB	Berkshire Hills Bancorp
BBY	Best Buy
BGCP	BGC Partners
BGFV	Big 5 Sporting Goods
BMR	Biomed Realty Trust
BKH	Black Hills
BKCC	Blackrock Kelso Capital
BLK	BlackRock
BX	Blackstone Group
BKEP	Blueknight Energy Partners
BNCN	BNC Bancorp
BWP	Boardwalk Pipeline Partners
BOWFF	Boardwalk REIT
BOKF	BOK Financial
TEU	Box Ships
BRC	Brady
BDN	Brandywine Realty Trust
BRE	BRE Properties
BBEP	BreitBurn Energy Partners
BGG	Briggs & Stratton
BMY	Bristol Myers Squibb
BR	Broadridge Financial Solutions

BIP	Brookfield Infrastructure Partners
BPO	Brookfield Office Properties
BRKL	Brookline Bancorp
BRKS	Brooks Automation (USA)
BMTC	Bryn Mawr Bank
BPL	Buckeye Partners
CA	CA Technologies
CVC	Cablevision Systems
CLMS	Calamos Asset Management
CWT	California Water Service Group
CALM	Cal-Maine Foods
CLMT	Calumet Specialty Products Partners
CPT	Camden Property Trust
CPB	Campbell Soup
CM	Canadian Imperial Bank of Commerce
CPLP	Capital Product Partners
CFFN	Capitol Federal Financial
CMO	Capstead Mortgage
CG	Carlyle Group
CCL	Carnival
CASC	Cascade
CATO	Cato
CBL	CBL & Associates Properties
CDI	CDI Corp.
CEC	CEC Entertainment
FUN	Cedar Fair
CDR	Cedar Realty Trust
CEL	Cellcom Israel
CVE	Cenovus Energy
CNP	CenterPoint Energy
CTL	CenturyLink
CRDN	Ceradyne
CHG	CH Energy Group
CHFC	Chemical Financial
CHMG	Chemung Financial
CHKE	Cherokee
CHKR	Chesapeake Granite Wash Trust

CHSP   Chesapeake Lodging Trust
CPK   Chesapeake Utilities
CVX   Chevron
CINF   Cincinnati Financial

Inside Trading Gone Wild

Some Brookers on Wall Street are still doing inside trading on Wall Street many people are saying. With experience traders, there is a lot of kiss and don't tell on Wall Street. Brookers and regular traders will not even tell their wives or close friends because they will not chance it of being found out

This inside trading activity will never stop. Inside trading may slow down at times but it is here to stay until God himself show-up.

What People Think about Mr. Jim Cramer

People are saying Jim Cramer is God gift to local stocks traders and I the writer of this book agree. He is honest and sincere

This man Mr. Cramer comes from humble beginning. He was at one time very poor but worked his way to the top, people are praising CNBC for having him. Jim Cramer has helped many people to become rich. What Ali was to boxing. Jim is to the stocks their may never be another person like Jim Cramer, from a scale from 1-10 we give him a ten.

CONCERNING BORROWING MONEY

Deuteronomy 15 Verse 6-13
Psalm 37, Verse 21—Proverbs 22, Verse 7

When we ask God for help, and when our help comes and we become Blessed, we usually forget where our help came from. Why when we borrow money we don't want to pay back that which we borrow. Even when God blessed us with enough so that we can pay back that which we borrow.

Should a person have to be economical so that they may have for tomorrow for themselves? YES

But why should they have to give to someone who had the same chance to store up and save for tomorrow but instead they spend their money lavishly, and without thinking of the future

THE DEVIL PRETENDS TO BE LIKE A LION

When the devil pretends to be like a lion, and when he is loosing his battle he likes to give his loudest roar. So don't be fooled by his loudest roar, because it is the beginning of your victory. God Bless Min. Titus Gay

HOLY BIBLE

Why God Holds Back His Blessings

In the old Testament Read
Haggai Chapter 1 Verse 4-10.

Is it time for you, O ye to dwell in your ceiled houses, and this house to lie waste now therefore thus saith the lord of host; consider your ways, ye have sown much and bring in little; ye eat; but ye have not filled with drink; ye clothe yourself, but there is none warm; and he that earneth wages to put in into a bag with holes, ye looked for much and to it came to little.

For example

If you give Ten dollars for a Godly cause, God will in return bless you many times over. All of your blessings that God gives you may not come in money. Some may come in a form of a better job, a better apartment, house or store. Someone may offer you a television set or some furniture, so we all must give so that God can let our blessing flow. For God loves a cheerful giver and some people always wonder why things become so hard for them but first they must ask themselves am I giving, when you be continuous in giving God will be continuous in blessing us, and he will make things better for you.

In the old TestamentMalachi
Chapter 3 Verse 10.

Bring ye all the tithes in to the storehouse, that there may be meat in mine house, and prove me now herewith, saith the Lord of hosts, if I will not open you the windows of heaven, and pour you out a blessing, that there shall not be room enough to receive it.

God want us to pay our tithes our 10% of our pay to be given to the church and he shall rain blessing upon us.

A PRAYER OF FORGIVENESS AND HEALING OF THE BODY
HIV & AIDS PRAYER

O' GOD of roaring power and mighty spirit, I ask of you to forgive me for my sins and cleanse my heart and purify my soul from all unrighteousness. O' GOD when I lift up my eyes towards the hill, my help will come. Remember me O' Lord and again I say please forgive me for my sins. For I will try harder to please you and try lesser to please man. Therefore O' GOD let my body be the temple of God and I will try to keep it clean that you may dwell in it. O' GOD I pray that you will let me live long that I may praise you and rejoice over you for many years to come. O' Lord I am no use to you in the grave, for I can't praise you in the grave, I can't rejoice over you in the grave. I ask of you to give me a chance O' Mighty God, please strengthen my heart and heal my HIV, or AIDS, that I may be able to go to the house of god every Sunday, let me praise you with comfortable feeling, for it is better to praise god with sweet feeling than in pain and uncomfortable feelings because of my HIV & AIDS. Therefore I ask of you in Jesus name heal me O' Lord I pray this day. O' GOD you have said seek and ye shall find and ask that it may be given, therefore I ask of you to give me good health, by healing my HIV & AIDS and give me a chance to not only worship you with good feelings, but go out and win souls. This is my pray to you O' GOD.

Written By Titus Gay

This is the Aids
Symbol. A jelly
like head with
roots with
variation of colors
as I saw in my sleep

Donation Accepted But Not Necessary
For free Bibles
Write: Titus Gay
         P.O. Box 781
         Sebring, FL 33871

What is Aids or Hiv?

Aids are excessive pollution of the body. Because the body is unable to fight off this excessive pollution it becomes a virus. AIDS is a form of cancer.

If a person use crack or inject themselves with drugs often. The body will become very polluted, and will not be able to fight off all of this pollution. Therefore it will afflict the body in the form of Cancer or Aids. If two men have unprotected sex and they constantly discharging in each other very often this can create bacteria in the butt area that can eventually lead to aids.

Vaccine

Vaccine may be the unsuspected killer that may be handed down to the second and third generation. It may not affect us but our grand children. Vaccine may cause *Cancer or Aids* unto the second or third generation.

? This is only my opinion

In my sleep I saw the Cure for Aids

In the middle of the night while I was asleep, my spirit went forth. To seek out a cure for AIDS. As my spirit was traveling, I look ahead and I saw a tree that grows mostly in the deep south in the U.S.A. and a plant that grows mostly in Southern Europe. I believe by extracting juices from the tree and plants, we will have the cure for Aids. I believe the plant is use to cut off the spread of Aids and the tree can be used to kill the Aids & HIV Virus.

This is the Aids
Symbol. A jelly
like head with
roots with
variation of colors
as I saw in my sleep

Researchers—can write me to find out about these plants:
Write to: Titus Gay
        Po. Box 781
        Sebring FL 33871

Mr. Booker Hannible
People call him the greatest unknown rapper
For info: Iambosb@email.com

Many people want to know what ever happen to Titus Gay, Sr
He is now 54 years old and is doing Great
His current photo below

At age 18 was New York finest Body Builders

Lazzzy Bum

Lazzzybum.com

Watching a movie? Want a cookie? Will get it for you.

Need a haircut? How about getting your haircut done by an
Emmy Award Winning Stylist.

Lazzzy Bum is an errand service. If you don't have the time or are just plain
lazy contact Lazzzy Bum for your needs. The best part of using our service is
that there are no commitments, you can name your own price and have your
task done in a timely fashion with no stress. It's that simple. Services available
are grocery shopping, haircuts at your home or office, sitting with your elderly
parent, personal training, etc. We stand out from our competition by our prices,
expertise and our constant improvement to meet our customer needs.

Phone: 863.443.6473 Email: info@lazzzybum.com

Passion for Jesus

If you don't believe that Jesus is the son of God or Jesus is the Messiah you can prove it by pray I have already prove it here is what you could say but first go in a private room by yourself or with someone who also want to prove Jesus existence and get serious and pray from the hart you could say Jesus I don't know you but I want to know if you are the Massiah or the son of God, I want to communicate with you, my family or parents never tell me of you but I want to reach out to you, Jesus reach out to me that I may know you, some time Jesus may come in a vision or a dream at night, sometimes he may show Himself in spirit form this have already happen to thousands of people even some Muslims, Hindus and also some Jews, Benny Hinn the preacher who apparently did believe that Jesus is the Massiah. I must say that millions of people witness Benny Hinn calling on Jesus in pray and the dum speak, the blind see and cancer disappear.

O God, Forgive us for our
Raging Passion for Women!
O GOD, FORGIVE US FOR OUR RAGING PASSION
FOR WOMEN!

O, how beautiful the women of the earth!

O God, because the craftiness and architectural work of your hands are so great by which you have made women, with wisdom and honor, many men of the earth have become beside themselves at the mere sight of a woman. Our hearts beat faster with excitement and our eyes often stare without ceasing. O God, have mercy upon us because of our uncontrollable passion for women. I praise Thee, O God, for the craftiness by which you have made woman but we need Thy help O Lord, to control ourselves. Let Thy mercy rain on us and Thy forgiveness be with us that we may better ourselves.

by T. Gay
Distributed by Praise of Israel Inc. 1998.

Cut back on your medication

(Blood Pressure)   Lime & Garlit—reduce your Blood pressure
Lime & Garlit—Help Regulate your *Blood*
Sugar diabetes—papaya—Alavara Juice
Fever—Lamon Grass
Hart problem—An Aspiran a day
        please see your doctor

stop vomoting we have this product write—T Gay
        PO. Box 781
        Sebring FL 33871
        Need Investors to promote this product
For pain   omega 3 3 times a day
        Soak in hot water for back & feet

For all problem seek God

Donna's Business Ad
3/3/2013 11:26:42 P.M. Eastern Standard Time
Dclairejam@aol.com

Have a fabulous day!
Donna Dedier-James
www.smartchoice.grid.net
www.wilaf.com

        We have many natural products
        for your health

ISAAC Gay became a stocks trader at 16 years of age and now at 24 yrs old, he consider himself to be an expert. I *ISAAC* Gay highly recommend this book

New York & Sebring FL
Rising Star Actor
And also work as a model
ISAAC Gay

ISAAC ESAU GAY
SAG AFTRA

isaacesaugay@isaacesaugay.com
www.isaacesaugay.com
http://www.imdb.me/isaacesaugay

My Take On The Market & Ways To Make Money

By Isaac Esau Gay

(Independent Investor & Owner of Lazzzybum.com)

Why Invest In Stocks

The possibilities of making money in a short time with the ability to buy or sell when you want to is phenomenal. Many new investors feel that the stocks market is a risk. In a sense yes and no. But if you think about it; Every decision in life is a risk. Getting married and your spouse develops cancer, having kids and they turn to drugs or going to college and graduating without a job in your field. There is always risk. But no risk no reward. The great thing about the stocks market is that you can study past trends. History repeats itself so does the market.

The stocks market is known to outperform most financial instruments. It outperforms savings accounts, cds, bonds, and money market funds. When you buy a stocks you can make money when the price increases and when a dividend yield is declared. What is a stocks dividend? A form of cash paid in stocks. It's when companies distribute a portion of its company's earnings to shareholder.

The best dividend stocks are Blue Chip stocks. And the reason being is because blue chips stocks are dinosaur companies. Companies that have a track record of 50 years plus.

With all that Information you can decipher and understand what season would be the best time to invest in that particular company.

A list of dividend stocks with great price appreciation:

> Con Edison (ED) Dividend Yield as of 3/2013 **4.19%**
> Exxon Mobil (XOM) Dividend Yield as of 3/2013 **2.57%**
> Apple (AAPL) Dividend Yield as of 3/2013 **2.33%**
> Visa (V) Dividend Yield as of 3/2013 **0.84%**
> Waste Management (WT) Dividend Yield as of 3/2013 **3.89%**
> Wal-Mart (WMT) Dividend Yield as of 3/2013 **2.59%**

Stock Evaluation

1) Purchase stocks with each of the last four years earning 30% or more.
2) Previous quarterly earnings and sales should be up at least 20%.
3) Avoid penny stocks.
4) Buy stocks selling higher than $25.
5) Cut Loses at 10%. Sell even if you feel it may go higher. Keep your emotions in check.
6) Look for big volume increases on charts.
7) Purchases companies when management owns stocks.
8) Always find out if a company is introducing a new product, new service or is under new management.
9) Buy Leaders
10) Stay away from technology stocks if you are conservative investor (Apple is an exception)
11) Read stocks market books on fundamental and technical analysis
12) Always check the market indexes daily
13) Never guess be sure!
14) Check supply and demands.
15) Create selling and buying rules and stick to them.
16) Best investment website for news and research are etrade.com, nasdq.com or cnbc.com
17) Buy the Wall Street Journal to be informed of the market.

Success in the stocks market doesn't happen overnight, but keep reading books and follow these stocks evaluation rules. You will have a better grasp on the market and will be able to multiply your earnings. There are many opportunities to learn about the stocks. Attend market seminars and meetings. If you don't live in any major city; there's live seminars online that will be at your disposable. In order to invest in the stocks market you have to generate income first. Below will be some tips on how to save money and how to generate extra income.

Live infomercials $500-$750 per week

A live infomercial is a short or regular-length live program that combines information presentation with an integrated suggestion to buy a particular product or service.

http://www.jescojobs.com/

Work As An Extra On Movies $85 to $500 a day

Background actor or extra is a performer in a film, television show, stage, musical, opera or ballet production, who appears in a nonspeaking, nonsinging or nondancing capacity, usually in the background (for example, in an audience or busy street scene). War films and epic films often employ background actors in large numbers

http://www.centralcasting.com/NY/actors/index.html
http://gwcnyc.com/casting.shtml
http://www.candccasting.com/
http://www.bgroundinc.com/index.htm

101 WAYS TO MAKE MONEY ONLINE

Every day more and more people are looking to learn how to make money fast.

LEGITIMATE WORK FROM HOME OPPORTUNITIES

Leave your office and work from home!

https://www.alpineaccess.com/
http://www.workingsolutions.com/
http://www.liveops.com/

Cater Waiter $15 hr. or more

A waiter is a person who works in either the catering or restaurant industry, and is invaluable to the food service process.

http://www.abigailkirsch.com/
http://www.aysstaff.com/
http://www.marceybrownstein.com/
http://www.benjamincateringny.com/
http://www.nyccateringcompany.com/
http://www.topshelfstaffers.com/

Focus Groups $100 to $2,000 flat rates

A **focus group** is a form of qualitative research in which a group of people are asked about their perceptions, opinions, beliefs and attitudes towards a product, service, concept, advertisement, idea, or packaging. Questions are asked in an interactive group setting where participants are free to talk with other group members. Basically, Get paid to share your opinion.

http://www.cash4talk.com/index.php
http://www.focusgroup.com/
http://www.iopinion.com/
http://www.sismarketresearch.com/join-focus-groups.html
http://www.probemarket.com/part_reg.php
http://www.fgglobal.com/

Ways to Make Extra Money

Promotional Modeling $15 hr. to $50 hr.

A promotional model is a model hired to drive consumer demand for a product, service, brand, or concept by directly interacting with potential consumers. A vast majority of promotional models are female and typically is intended to be attractive in physical appearance. They serve to provide information about the product or service and make it appealing to consumers. While the length of interaction may be short, the promotional model delivers a live experience that reflects on the product or service he or she is representing.

http://www.attackmarketing.net/login.php
https://talent.proplusleads.com/reg.aspx
http://www.fusioneventstaffing.com/talent.php
http://www.8dayspromotions.com/contact.html
http://thehypeagency.com/talent-registration/
http://www.victory-agency.com/
http://login.gcmarketingservices.com/frontend/register.php
http://www.encorenationwide.com/
http://www.michael-alan.com/
http://www.boomfitness.com/jobs2.html

Night chaperon $10 hr. or more

An adult who accompanies or supervises young people on social occasions

http://sdprotection.com/contact.php

Saving

1) Get rid of your debt. The only thing debt is good for is creating more of it. Pay off your debt immediately. Set up a payment plan as soon as possible with your bank. Having a credit card is good to have to show a company if you can pay payments on time. My suggestion is to use your credit card for necessities for example grocery shopping, gas, household items, etc. Things you need to survive. Things you want use cash; because as the cash goes you realize this is not good idea. Seeing is believing and seeing your cash dwindling down will make you more financial conscious. We all want to be in a better position but the main thing to remember that you are progressing.

2) Create an emergency fund of $10,000 or more. Set saving goals is a must. Five hundred dollars month for 2 years can bring you over $10k in savings. Have short, mid and long-term goals.

3) Save your receipts and record expenses. Buy a notebook and list how much you make and how much you spend. Be detailed and never leave out small purchases.

4) Create a budget for yourself and family.

5) When you receive money immediately pay your self-first. You can set up automatic transfer from your checking account into your saving account. Also set up a direct deposit at your job that will help as well.

www.ingramcontent.com/pod-product-compliance
Lightning Source LLC
Chambersburg PA
CBHW022112170526
45157CB00004B/1590